Grading Visible Learners

Dedications

From Dave:

This book is dedicated to my family. It is through their steadfast support, understanding, and strength that I have reached this stage in my career. Kristen, you are an incredible partner, a loving wife, and a devoted mother—I am truly fortunate to have you in my life! Nicholas, Zachary, and Jacob, you have all grown into remarkable young men who bring me immense pride and serve as a true inspiration. I can't wait to see the man each of you is going to become. I am deeply grateful to all three of you for your unwavering love and patience—and heaven knows Dad doesn't have a lot of patience. . . . So I thank you from the bottom of my heart for yours!

From Bruce:

This book is dedicated to my family. It has only been with their unwavering understanding, support, and strength that I have arrived at this point in my career. Rebecca, you are a tremendous partner, a wonderful wife, and dedicated mother—I am so lucky! Jaxen and Landon, you both have become tremendous men who are not only my pride and joy but a true inspiration to me. I must thank all three of you for your constant love and patience. I love you!

Grading Visible Learners

Learning With Fluidity, Not Finality

Dave Nagel

Bruce Potter

Foreword by John Almarode

Afterword by John Hattie

FOR INFORMATION:

Corwin
A SAGE Company
2455 Teller Road
Thousand Oaks, California 91320
(800) 233-9936
www.corwin.com

SAGE Publications Ltd.
1 Oliver's Yard
55 City Road
London EC1Y 1SP
United Kingdom

SAGE Publications India Pvt. Ltd.
Unit No 323-333, Third Floor, F-Block
International Trade Tower Nehru Place
New Delhi 110 019
India

SAGE Publications Asia-Pacific Pte. Ltd.
18 Cross Street #10-10/11/12
China Square Central
Singapore 048423

Vice President and
 Editorial Director: Monica Eckman
Senior Publisher: Jessica Allan
Senior Content
 Development Editor: Mia Rodriguez
Production Editor: Tori Mirsadjadi
Copy Editor: Michelle Ponce
Typesetter: C&M Digitals (P) Ltd.
Cover Designer: Scott Van Atta
Marketing Manager: Olivia Bartlett

Copyright © 2025 by Corwin Press, Inc.

All rights reserved. Except as permitted by U.S. copyright law, no part of this work may be reproduced or distributed in any form or by any means, or stored in a database or retrieval system, without permission in writing from the publisher.

When forms and sample documents appearing in this work are intended for reproduction, they will be marked as such. Reproduction of their use is authorized for educational use by educators, local school sites, and/or noncommercial or nonprofit entities that have purchased the book.

All third-party trademarks referenced or depicted herein are included solely for the purpose of illustration and are the property of their respective owners. Reference to these trademarks in no way indicates any relationship with, or endorsement by, the trademark owner.

Apple Core Icon from istock.com/arcady_31 and Second Chances icon from istock.com/dinosoftlabs

Paperback ISBN 978-1-0719-3429-6

DISCLAIMER: This book may direct you to access third-party content via web links, QR codes, or other scannable technologies, which are provided for your reference by the author(s). Corwin makes no guarantee that such third-party content will be available for your use and encourages you to review the terms and conditions of such third-party content. Corwin takes no responsibility and assumes no liability for your use of any third-party content, nor does Corwin approve, sponsor, endorse, verify, or certify such third-party content.

Contents

ONLINE APPENDIX CONTENTS — ix

FOREWORD BY JOHN ALMARODE — xi

ACKNOWLEDGMENTS — xv

ABOUT THE AUTHORS — xvii

PART I: SETTING THE STAGE FOR GRADING TO DEVELOP GREAT LEARNERS — 1

CHAPTER 1: CHANGING THE NARRATIVE OF GRADING FROM FINALITY TO FLUIDITY — 3
- Aligning Grading With Learning — 5
- Effective Grading Is Not a Game or a Crap Shoot — 8

CHAPTER 2: DEVELOPING VISIBLE LEARNERS THROUGH GRADING — 13
- Developing Great *Learners* — 14
- Overview of the Six Traits of a *Visible Learner*, Who Drives Their Own Learning — 15
- G.R.A.D.E.S — 17

CHAPTER 3: CHALLENGES TO GRADING VISIBLE LEARNERS — 21
- 1. Traditions Trumping Evidence — 22
- 2. Commonly Held Beliefs — 25
- 3. Absence of Collaboration Around Grading — 29
- 4. (Too Much) of a Focus on Grading Process Criteria — 29
- 5. Not Considering Cognitive Engagement — 30

CHAPTER 4: CORE GRADING ACTIONS AND THE SI²TE MODEL — 33
- Core Practice 1: Teacher Collaboration — 34
- Core Practice 2: Clarity of Scoring — 39
- Core Practice 3: Collaborative Scoring and Feedback of Student Work — 40

Core Practice 4: Multiple Opportunities for Success Through Stipulated Second Chances	42
Stipulated Second Chances	43
Gather the Right Evidence	47

CHAPTER 5: MINDFRAMES AND BELIEFS DRIVE ACTIONS TO IMPACT STUDENT LEARNING — 49

Beliefs Drive Actions	50

CHAPTER 6: BRINGING CLARITY TO GRADING — 55

Clarity of Grading Scoring Guide	55
How Students Learn	58
Mindframes for Learning	59
Visible Learner Trait to Be Developed	59
Designing Generative Learning Experiences	59
Making Quality Inferences From Eliciting the Best Evidence	60
Weighted Scoring	61
Rigor and Complexity as the Guide	63
Better Alignment Between Classroom Grades and Standardized Assessments	63
CGSG—A Strong Counselor, Not Jailor	64

PART II: CLASSROOM AND PLC ACTIONS TO DEVELOP EACH OF THE 6 TRAITS OF A VISIBLE LEARNER THROUGH GRADING — 67

CHAPTER 7: GREAT LEARNERS GAUGE THEIR CURRENT LEVEL OF UNDERSTANDING — 69

Commonly Held Grading Beliefs	71
Multiple Levels of Clarity to Consider	76
Applying the Clarity of Grading Scoring Guide to the Previous Scenario	77
Use Metacognition to Monitor Progress	81
Assessing in Advance of Instruction	82

CHAPTER 8: GREAT LEARNERS ARE READY TO TAKE ON CHALLENGES — 85

Setting Goals and Achieving Personal Bests Versus Performance Goals	88
Success Criteria as *the* Catalyst	91
Aligning Success Criteria to Mastery Grading	94
Mastery Learning	95
Mastery Grading	97
Using Grading to Inform Next Learning Steps	102
Success Criteria: For Desired Behaviors	104

CHAPTER 9: GREAT LEARNERS ADAPT TOOLS TO GUIDE THEIR LEARNING — 107
- Alignment to Success Criteria Is Critical — 109
- Supporting Students in Adapting Tools to Guide Their Learning — 114
- Self-Judgment and Reflection — 115
- Avoid Early Grading — 118
- Training Tasks — 118
- Training Tasks as an Initial Assessment Tool and De-Stressor — 118

CHAPTER 10: GREAT LEARNERS DETERMINE HOW TO SEEK FEEDBACK AND RECOGNIZE ERRORS ARE OPPORTUNITIES TO LEARN — 123
- Report Cards *Can* Lead to Hodgepodge Grading — 126
- Feedback Should Align With, Not Oppose Grading Actions — 131
- Single Point Rubrics — 134
- Feedback Doesn't Know if It's Practice or a Game — 138
- Going Deeper With Feedback — 140

CHAPTER 11: GREAT LEARNERS EVALUATE THEIR PROGRESS — 147
- Opening Prose — 147
- Potential Pitfalls — 151
- Actions to Promote Students Monitoring Progress — 154

CHAPTER 12: GREAT LEARNERS ARE SUCCESSFUL IN RECOGNIZING THEIR LEARNING AND TEACH OTHERS — 167
- Supporting Students to Respond to Current Results — 170
- Peer Tutoring — 173
- Peer and Self Grading — 176
- Grading Behaviors of Visible Learners—Collaboration — 178

CHAPTER 13: EFFECTIVE GRADING IS A CRITICAL COMPONENT OF THE PRACTICE OF TEACHING — 185
- Develop Great Learners, Not Good Students — 186
- Apply the Mindframes for Learning — 187
- Implement Core Grading Actions — 187
- Utilize the SI^{2}TE Model — 188
- Conclusion — 190

AFTERWORD BY JOHN HATTIE — 193

REFERENCES — 197

INDEX — 203

Online Appendix Contents

Appendix 1: Self-Review Tool: Grading Visible Learners

Appendix 2: Master List of Commonly Held Beliefs

Appendix 3: Master List of Concepts, Frameworks, and Strategies

Appendix 4: Applying the SI^{2}TE Model

Appendix 5: Grading Strategies Tied to SI^{2}TE Model and Mindframes

Appendix 6: Stipulated Second Chance Contract

Appendix 7: Protocol for Analyzing Assignments and Tasks for Alignment to Standards and Success Criteria

Appendix 8: Student Goal Setting Template

Appendix 9: Agreement on *Truthful* Grading Using a Reading Anchor Standard as Example

Appendix 10: Examples of Learner Dispositions

Appendix 11: Assignment/Task Reflection Tool

Appendix 12: Sample Report Card Examples

Appendix 13: Collaborative Feedback Tool

Appendix 14: Elementary Math Example

Appendix 15: Amnesty Day Menu

Appendix 16: Group Roles

Visit the companion website at
https://companion.corwin.com/courses/GradingVisibleLearners
for the downloadable resources listed above.

Note From the Publisher: The authors have provided web content in this book that is available to you through QR (quick response) codes. To read a QR code, you must have a smartphone or tablet with a camera. We recommend that you download a QR code reader app that is made specifically for your phone or tablet brand.

Foreword

I remember it as if it were yesterday. My professor, who will remain anonymous, handed back a test in one of my college mathematics courses. On the top in bright red ink was the number 42. Yes, I had earned 42 of the 100 possible points on the test. My professor gently said to me, "Mr. Almarode, I assume I will see you during office hours this week." My professor was right, I would be visiting him during office hours that week and for the remaining weeks of the semester. However, as I walked to his office to meet with him, I had no idea what I was going to say or ask. While I clearly failed the test and did not have an acceptable grasp of the content, I could not articulate where I was going in my learning, how I was progressing in my learning, and where I needed to go next to close the gap in my learning. The grade of 42 told me nothing other than that I had only earned 42 percent of the possible points on the test. The 42 percent told me that I had failed the test. What that grade meant for me as a learner, the information communicated by that particular grade, was simply that I had earned an F. This begs the question, what is a grade? What purpose does it serve in teaching and learning? Are grades helpful in teaching and learning?

Grades have long been a cornerstone of educational systems, serving as shorthand for what students know and how well they perform. Yet, for many educators, students, and families, grades evoke complex feelings: pride, frustration, confusion, or even anxiety. In this landscape, where the meaning of grades can sometimes feel elusive or arbitrary, Dave Nagel and Bruce Potter provide an essential guide to understanding how grades, when used thoughtfully and intentionally, can become powerful tools for learning.

At their best, grades are more than symbols on a report card—they are a form of communication. A well-constructed grade should not merely categorize performance but illuminate understanding and provide a path forward (e.g., where am I going in my learning, how am I progressing in my learning, and where do I need to go next to close the gap). Dave and Bruce remind us that grades can be a bridge between where learners are now and where they are headed. This perspective, rooted in research and shaped by years of classroom experience, challenges us to think differently about grading. Instead of treating grades as the end point of learning, they invite us to view them as one of many sources of feedback that guide students toward growth: learning with fluidity, not finality.

This book is a timely and much-needed contribution to the ongoing conversation about evaluation in education. What is most impressive about this book is that Dave and Bruce do not shy away from the complexities of grading, nor do they offer quick fixes or one-size-fits-all solutions. Instead, they equip us with practical tools and nuanced perspectives, grounded in both evidence and empathy, to navigate the challenges of grading in ways that move student learning forward.

One of the book's most powerful arguments is its assertion that grading should serve learning rather than overshadow it. Too often, grades are wielded as tools of compliance, used to rank or punish rather than to support. The authors challenge us to reframe grading as a process that fosters growth and self-reflection. They show how clear, consistent, and fair grading practices can enhance students' understanding of their strengths and areas for improvement, empowering them to take an active role in their own learning journey.

The authors also emphasize the relational aspect of grading. Effective grading is not an isolated act; it is part of a larger ecosystem of feedback, communication, and trust. By aligning grading practices with learning intentions and success criteria and creating opportunities for dialogue about what grades mean, we can build stronger partnerships with our students and their families. These partnerships, in turn, deepen everyone's investment in the learning process.

What sets this work apart is its commitment to bridging theory and practice. The authors delve into a wide array of research on grading and feedback, distilling complex findings into clear and actionable insights. This synthesis is no small feat. While the academic literature on grading is vast, much of it remains inaccessible to those working on the front lines of education. Instead, we are left in the middle of grading policy battles where teaching and learning are collateral damage. By translating this body of research into practical strategies, Dave and Bruce ensure that we can not only understand the principles of effective grading but also apply them in our classrooms.

As you turn these pages, you will find a wealth of strategies for implementing grading practices that are transparent, equitable, and purposeful. You will encounter stories from classrooms where grading has been transformed from a source of frustration into a catalyst for growth. You will be guided through practical steps for aligning grading policies with the principles of effective feedback, ensuring that your practices support—not hinder—learning.

But this book does more than provide guidance; it inspires reflection. It challenges educators to examine their own assumptions about grading and to ask critical questions: What do my grades communicate? Do they reflect what students have truly learned? How can I ensure that my grading practices promote equity and opportunity? These questions are not always easy to answer, but they are essential for fostering a culture of learning that values progress over performance.

What makes this work so compelling is the authors' unwavering belief in the potential of all learners and the potential for grades to be an essential part of the learning process. This belief is woven through every chapter, infusing their recommendations with a sense of purpose and possibility. They remind us that grading, when done well, is not just about assigning a number or a letter. It is about helping students see their own growth and inspiring them to reach their next level of understanding.

The authors of this book are more than educators; they are advocates for a better, more equitable system of evaluation. They advocate for schools and classrooms where a 42 percent tells the learner where they are going, how they are progressing, and what they need to do to close the gap. Their insights, drawn from research and practice, are a gift to anyone seeking to make grading a meaningful and constructive part of education. Whether you are an experienced teacher looking to refine your practices, a school leader seeking to implement systemwide change, or a new educator grappling with the complexities of evaluation, this book offers both guidance and hope.

As you embark on this journey, know that you are not alone. The questions and challenges you face are shared by educators around the world. But with the tools and perspectives offered here, you will be equipped to turn grading into a force for good—a process that supports learning, inspires growth, and communicates possibility.

Grading, done right, can be transformative. Again, learning with fluidity, not finality. This book shows us how.

—John Almarode, Associate Professor of Education,
James Madison University

Acknowledgments

From Dave:

Getting to a successful place in your career never happens without support, a little bit of luck, as well as others who have supported and shaped you. I am extremely grateful for being able to earn a master's degree from Butler University's Experiential Program for Preparing School Principals (EPPSP Group 17), where I learned from Dr. Steve Heck what it really means to be a true leader. I would like to thank Jeff Hubble, my first principal when I became a building administrator. Jeff taught me the value of teamwork and making sure that if you would not expose your own children to an environment, then you should not allow someone else there without trying to make it better. I would like to thank Dr. B. R. Jones, superintendent of Jones County schools in Mississippi. He has been a dear friend and colleague of mine for over a decade, and he is my *Ambassador of Quan!* Next, I would like to thank Bruce—without you with me on this journey, my vision for this book would have never come to fruition. Thanks, as well, to Jessica Allan, our editor, and Mia Rodriguez for all your support. And finally, my dad, Ken Nagel, who alone taught me that you cannot live if you are *Standing OUTSIDE the fire!*

From Bruce:

You don't get anywhere in your life traveling alone. Over a 30-year career working in multiple schools serving in multiple roles, you are bound to experience success and failure. I've had many wonderful people positively influence my growth and development. I'd like to give a special acknowledgement to three influential colleagues: Christine Burke, Dan Kalbliesh, and Cathy O'Brien, as well as three influential mentors: Wayne Bertrand, Lee Bordick, and Mike Ford. The six of you have been by my side; keeping me humble during the success, and picking me up during the challenges—sincerely, thank you!

Publisher's Acknowledgments

Corwin gratefully acknowledges the contributions of the following reviewers:

Alisa Barrett
Director of Instruction
Greenfield Exempted Village Schools
Greenfield, Ohio

Mike Ford
Educational Consultant
New York State Council of School Superintendents
Albany, NY

B. R. Jones
Superintendent of Education and Former international Visible Learning Consultant
Jones County School District
Ellisville, Mississippi

Dan Kalbfliesh
Superintendent of Schools
Green Island UFSD
New York, NY

O'Shean Moran
Principal
Billings Public Schools
Billings, MT

Ken O'Connor
Consultant and Author
AFS Inc
Toronto, Ontario

Jenny Starr
Science Teacher, Middle School
Green Island UFSD
Green Island, NY

Krista Thomsen
Director of Curriculum, Instruction, and Assessment
Lancaster School District
Lancaster, CA

About the Authors

Dave Nagel has been a professional developer and educational consultant both nationally and internationally since 2003 and has done so as his primary job in education since 2008. Prior to that, he was a middle and high school science teacher and administrator in a large district in Indianapolis. As a school leader at Ben Davis High School (enrollment 3,000 students), Dave was instrumental in developing a focused plan for differentiated goals for students based on specific proficiency measures that supported the school in improving its graduation rate 14 percent in just over four years.

Dave's primary areas of expertise are in the areas of effective teacher and leader collaboration, assessment and feedback, and, specifically, effective grading actions both at the school and classroom level. He has been working specifically with Professor John Hattie's Visible Learning research since 2011, which is a driving force for all of his work with teachers, coaches, and administrators. He has authored five books previous to this one, including four within the *PLC+* series of publications (Corwin). He has also published multiple times in various publications such as *Principal Leadership* and *Educational Leadership* and has also presented at various national conferences.

Dave has a strong moral aspect, strives to be very relatable and practical when working with people, and has a savvy sense of humor that supports him in his life and work. Dave stays very busy with his beautiful and supportive wife, Kristen, and three boys (ages 20, 15, and 13). He acknowledges every day that the Lord guides his actions and is the driving force in his life. Dave is an independent consultant for Corwin and is the owner of NZJ Learning LLC (named after his three boys) and the founder of the Center for Collaborative Expertise.

Bruce Potter is a school administrator with over thirty years of experience. Bruce began his career as a classroom teacher and has held leadership roles at the building level as a principal and at the district level as a superintendent for eleven years. In 2013, he secured special legislation that was signed into law by the governor of New York to open a public school for at-risk and special education students who were identified by their home districts as future high school dropouts. Over a six-year period, they achieved a graduation rate of 80 percent. In his current role, he is leading his district's certification as a Visible Learning school through the implementation of effective PLCs. Over the course of his career, he has shared his district's successes at several national conferences. Bruce is an independent consultant for Corwin and is cofounder of the Center for Collaborative Expertise.

Part I

Setting the Stage for Grading to Develop Great Learners

CHAPTER 1

Changing the Narrative of Grading From Finality to Fluidity

"The measure of intelligence is the ability to change"

—Albert Einstein

Consider the following scenarios where a student comes home from school and engages with their parents over dinner talking about what happened in school that day.

SCENARIO 1	SCENARIO 2
The classroom buzzed as students packed up at the end of the day. Mrs. Smith scanned the room for lingering questions, noting both excitement and anxiety about the upcoming math test. **Mrs. Smith:** Hey Sam, can I see you for a moment? **Sam** (hunched over notes): What's up, Mrs. Smith? **Mrs. Smith:** You seem stressed about tomorrow's test. Is that what's wrong?	In the days leading up to the unit test, Mrs. Smith stood at the front of the classroom with a detailed outline of the criteria students would be assessed on displayed prominently behind her. **Mrs. Smith:** Okay, class, today we're going to review exactly what you need to know for the upcoming exam. This test will gauge your understanding of key concepts from our unit, and I want to ensure that everyone knows what they need to do to prepare. Note the criteria from the unit displayed on the whiteboard:

(Continued)

(Continued)

SCENARIO 1	SCENARIO 2
Sam: I'm worried about my grade. I've studied, but I think I'll get a D **Mrs. Smith:** Only a D? You know I'm offering extra assignments to boost your grade if you struggle, right? Just put in some effort and get those completed and in by next Friday. **Sam:** Yeah, I know, but it's tough to focus on all that we have covered in this unit. **Mrs. Smith:** I want you to focus on studying the key concepts, but everything we have covered is important. How well you do matters a lot related to your grade, so all is fair game for the test. Do your best, and no matter what, keep track of those extra assignments, and you'll be alright. *Remember, every point counts so let's make a plan to get those assignments in on time!* **Sam** (nodded): I'll do my best, and either way I'll finish those extra tasks by the deadline for sure. **Mrs. Smith** (smiling sympathetically): I know you will, a good grade shows your effort. Just aim for that B. As they returned to the chaotic classroom, Sam felt the weight of his grades pressing down even more. His focus shifted from studying and preparing for the test to figuring out how and when he would complete the additional assignments.	• Define and be able to interpret essential terms such as photosynthesis and cellular respiration • Explain their processes and draw comparisons between them Expect multiple-choice questions on vocabulary, short answer questions focused on the functions of plant and animal cells. And some open-ended questions and prompts for you to articulate understanding of the stages of photosynthesis and cellular respiration in your own words. *(Mrs. Smith refers as well to her grading criteria for the assessment)* As you can see, your grade will reflect what you are able to demonstrate in your learning. Sam, a student who sometimes is a little lazy but tries hard to be prepared for tests and thrives in environments where expectations are made clear, says to himself, "Ok, I feel good about photosynthesis but not as much about cellular respiration. And I feel pretty good about being able to decipher what's being asked on multiple choice questions but less so when it comes to explaining my thinking in short responses." To provide a little more clarity, Mrs. Smith held up a sample question. **Mrs. Smith:** For instance, a short-answer question might ask you to describe the role of chlorophyll. It's crucial that you can explain how it functions in the process, rather than just listing what it is. You will also need to label the parts of a cell and provide brief descriptions of their functions. Sam felt a little bit better knowing that he would be expected to label the parts of the cell but less confident about being able to provide descriptions. **Mrs. Smith:** Remember learning is a journey, and Monday's test is a rest stop to see where we are. Yes, there will be a grade, but remember—that grade tells us where we need to go next. We will go back through the test afterward to see where we need to focus next during our science learning expedition.
Sam Goes Home Monday After the Test	**Sam Goes Home Monday After the Test**

SCENARIO 1	SCENARIO 2
Parent: Sam, how did you do on your test? **Sam:** Not very well, I think I got a D. **Parent:** Oh no, did you study? **Sam:** Yes, but not that hard because we are never sure what is going to be on the test. Mrs. Smith said if I do a few extra assignments I can get the points back and still get a B. **Parent:** Whew! Ok then, as long as you can still get a B! Just make sure you get those assignments done and turned in. Pass the peas, please!	**Parent:** Sam, how did you do on your test? **Sam:** Not as well as I would have liked, but I knew going in I was likely going to struggle on some of the criteria that was going to be on it. **Parent:** So, what's next? What feedback did you get? **Sam:** Mrs. Smith had us go through the questions first to see what we got right and whether we thought the question or concept was easy or if we got it right because we worked hard on that question or idea. Then for what we got wrong, we had to figure out if it was stuff we know but need to practice and get feedback from her, or if it is stuff we still need her to reteach. **Parent:** That's awesome. Of course, we want you to get good grades, but making sure you are learning what you need to and how you are making a plan for where you need to go next in that class is most important. Please pass the peas, kiddo!

Both scenarios are hypothetical but far from fictitious. Scenario 1 is unfortunately much more common and is the result of grades being viewed as *a symbol* to which meaning is attached and far too often not about learning and progress; rather, more of a prize to be attained than about what's next.

Scenario 2 is *not* Pollyanna. It is a glimpse into what we should espouse to create in every classroom where grades are used as a form of feedback to determine the next steps in learning. If we desire this to become the normal narrative related to grades with all stakeholders (students, parents, other educators, etc.), then we must commit to taking certain actions that lead to grades being viewed as an interval in the learning journey and not just the destination or prize at the end.

Aligning Grading With Learning

How would you describe learning in your school or classroom? What are the students doing? What is the teacher doing? Is it fluid and ongoing, or is it thought of as something that must stop at a specific point in time. like the end *of a lesson, week, unit, or semester?* Most, if not all, teachers talk about learning being a lifelong endeavor that never ends, never as an ultimate destination. Now, how would you describe grading in your school or classroom? Is there congruence between the two, or are they very dissimilar?

Grading actions are often the most misaligned strategies from research and evidence of any that take place in schools and are the most inconsistent of all practices from one classroom to another. We send so many mixed messages to our students on a regular basis by how we grade. Students are told to be curious, take risks, and have ownership of their learning, but then we implement a grading system that rewards and promotes a culture of completion compliance and, at times, punishes students when they do take risks and don't follow a predetermined path of learning. We teach them that they have to learn how to play a new grading game every year and sometimes from one hour to the next. This disrupts so many of the instructional, assessment, and affective actions of teachers who truly desire to have the greatest impact on the learning of their students.

This book *is* about improving grading approaches, actions, and practices while providing specific and concrete tools and strategies teachers and collaborative teams can adapt and use in their classrooms right away. It is also about empowering educators to maximize their impact by ensuring that grading serves as a constructive tool rather than a hindrance to student success.

This book is about how we *best impact the learning* of all students and develop them to be great learners in everything we do in our schools and classrooms. Unfortunately, grading actions far too often derail efforts to do so.

If we truly desire our students to view learning as an ongoing, never-ending journey, one that is fluid and moving versus one that is final, and to take more ownership, then certain mindsets and actions are called for:

1. Viewing grades as feedback
2. Ensuring clarity is the driver
3. Disrupting the culture of completion compliance
4. Having a formative mindset

Acknowledge That Grades Are a Form of Feedback

The two scenarios at the start of the chapter highlight contrasting views on grades. In the first, grades are seen as the result of actions that may not align with learning goals, resembling a game where students collect points for a reward. In the second, grades are viewed as feedback for learning, helping students bridge the gap between where they are and their goals. According to Winne and Butler (1994), feedback helps learners refine their knowledge and strategies. If teachers view grading actions with the same lens they do instructional feedback, we can shift students' focus from "What did I get?" to "Where do I go next?"

Clarity First and Above All Else

When students are asked, "How did you get that grade?" their common response is often, "I don't know!" They're not being dishonest; clarity is the missing link in grading. Future chapters emphasize the importance of clarity for both teachers and students, especially regarding expectations for learning, demonstration of that learning, and assessment methods. The grading aspect is frequently overlooked and is essential for changing the perception of grades as a final judgment on learning.

To facilitate this shift, teachers must clearly understand what they are teaching and ensure students grasp the intended learning outcomes. They need to be aware of potential learning progressions so students can see their path toward achieving goals. This knowledge empowers teachers to select effective assessment tools that accurately reflect student understanding and the rigor of tasks.

Additionally, collaboration in developing quality, rigorous tasks aligned with agreed-upon success criteria is crucial. Teachers must share the criteria for mastery and define what progress looks like at the start of learning cycles. This way, they can evaluate evidence of learning and make informed decisions about the next steps for their students.

Disrupting the Culture of Completion Compliance

One mindset we must dismantle in education through adult actions is the focus on simply completing tasks as students' primary goal. Consider this question: How often have you said, "I need my students to complete this task, assignment, homework, or lab," without explaining, or having thought through, *why?* Or, without communicating how that work aligns with specific learning goals or how it informs your instructional approach? How does it help students understand their next steps in learning?

We recognize that teachers face overwhelming demands and are often tasked with more than they can achieve in the time frames they are allotted. As a result, grading can become merely another item to check off, leading to a culture of *completion compliance*. Papers, tests, and essays are graded, entered in the gradebook, and returned to students, prompting the thought, "Whew, I'm finally caught up!" This reflects the historical habit of bribery as described by Jenkins (2021): If students submit their work, they receive credit.

Consequently, students then learn to view the completion and submission of assignments *as their ultimate goal*. They receive grades as a transaction: Timely work equals X amount of points or credit, while late submissions mean *X-minus*. This fosters a mindset of, "I'm done, what's my grade?" Parents reinforce this by telling their children to "make sure get your work done and handed in," totally emphasizing the completion over quality. This perspective halts the learning process, reducing education to a task that feels final once completed.

Having a Formative Mindset

Educators must recognize that a student's learning is ongoing and fluid, rather than a fixed endpoint. Educators with a *formative mindset* constantly recognize that all evidence they gather from their students, especially what they intentionally elicit, must primarily inform instructional actions aimed at helping students meet targeted objectives. This represents a significant shift from a more traditional view of ensuring that evidence in the form of scores is entered into a gradebook to track performance fairly. While grade recording isn't inherently bad, it should take a backseat to how teachers and students use that evidence to enhance learning. Many educators enter the field with an expert blind spot, assuming their own learning paths dictate how students should reach their goals. This perspective often prevents teachers from accurately diagnosing students' current learning stages and adjusting their instructional approaches accordingly (Nagel, 2015). When they embrace a mindset and always view evidence they gather formatively, to impact *their next instructional decision or approach,* they are much more keenly aware of how to best diagnose their students' next learning needs.

Effective Grading Is Not a Game or a Crap Shoot

Students learn to navigate the "game of school," structured by adult-established rules, which vary significantly between classrooms. Unfortunately, grades often reflect a student's ability to play this game rather than their actual learning (Scouller, 1998; Stanger-Hall, 2012; Towns & Robinson, 1993). There's no universal formula to enhance learning and achievement through grading; however, there are guiding principles.

Here in 2025, we have gained more evidence of effective practices that increase positive outcomes in education. We frequently reference Professor John Hattie's Visible Learning research, which highlights effective actions and approaches to consider and those to avoid. Grading practices are no exception and are often the most misaligned strategies from research and evidence of any that take place in schools and are the most inconsistent from one classroom to another.

Dr. Tom Guskey, a leading expert in grading research, and Susan Brookhart have synthesized over a century of grading research in their publication, *What We Know About Grading: What Works, What Doesn't, and What's Next* (Guskey & Brookhart, 2019).

Figure 1.1 is a snapshot of some research evidence that should impact our decision-making in schools and classrooms related to grading. We developed a question to consider before reading each statement or summary. Please read through them, and reflect on how each statement and the question posed currently does or could impact your or your schools' grading actions.

FIGURE 1.1: EXAMPLES OF EFFECTIVE GRADING RESEARCH AND CONSIDERATIONS

RESEARCH	CONSIDERATIONS FOR PRACTICE IN YOUR SCHOOL OR CLASSROOM
Do we prevent risk taking by grading early? High-achieving students on initial graded assignments appear somewhat sheltered from some of the negative impacts of grades, as they tend to maintain their interest in completing future assignments; presumably in anticipation of receiving additional good grades, but they may the lack the desire to take risks when success is not guaranteed (Butler, 1988).	• Keep students interested with challenging, meaningful tasks. • Encourage learning and experimentation to foster risk taking. • Use assessments and feedback to emphasize skill development and progress. • Design assignments that push creative and critical thinking. • Acknowledge high-quality work and effort, promoting persistence and resilience.
Do we confuse undesired behavior for a lack of achievement or aptitude? Students with disruptive behavior are 10 times more likely to have a gap between their achievement (grades) and their IQ (McCall et al., 1992; Guskey & Bailey, 2009).	• Separate behavior from grades to reflect true academic skills. • A gap between grades and IQ may signal unmet needs. • Offer clear feedback focused on academic improvement. • Address behavioral issues to minimize their impact on performance.
Do we enable behaviors and reward them in the form of academic grades? McMillan (2001) surveyed 1,483 classroom teachers in Grades 6-12. The researcher found effort and participation were the factors considered most often to determine a grade.	• Fairly assess these factors in grading. • Combine effort and participation with academic performance. • Clearly explain their impact on grades. • Use them to boost engagement, without compromising academic focus.
Do rigid mathematical formulas put students in a place to consider opting out of learning due to lack of potential reward? Oettinger (2002) and Grant and Green (2013) looked specifically for positive impacts of grades as incentives for students on the threshold between grade categories in a class. They hypothesized that, for example, a student on the borderline between a C and a D in a class would be more motivated to study for a final exam than a student solidly in the middle of the C range.	• Grades can motivate students near grade boundaries. • These students may be driven by the chance for a higher grade. • Use grade advancement as a motivation tool. • Assess if this strategy boosts outcomes without causing undue stress.
Are grades undesired carrots? Too often grades are the carrot intended to motivate students. We hear often that what used to motivate students doesn't anymore. Well, we believe it never really did, it was a game that fewer students in 2025 are interested in playing. In classrooms where grades are emphasized, students tend to attribute performance to ability rather than effort (Ames, 1992). Therefore, using grades as a carrot to promote effort may defeat the purpose (Guskey, 2019)!	• Grades may no longer effectively motivate students. • Emphasizing grades can shift focus to ability rather than effort. • Using grades just to motivate may undermine genuine effort.

Grades Are Not Evil and We Should Not Just Do Away With Them!—Our Goals for This Work

The challenges of grading have persisted for over a century (Starch & Elliott, 1912), with researchers offering ideas to address issues of validity and subjectivity but some saying it simply cannot be done. Some quip that transforming grading requires so many nuances, from policy development, to clear understanding by teachers, students, and parents, as well as to ensuring we have complete interrater reliability, and even then, there will still be challenges. However, teachers should not throw away their gradebooks, as some authors have suggested. We scoff at approaches like this as they would likely harm students and, in most districts, would be a termination offense.

Our goal in putting this work together is for educators, parents, and stakeholders to begin to view grades as part of students' learning journeys rather than as final judgments. This is not to create the notion of eliminating the importance of scores from tests and quizzes, which are vital in the classroom. While summative grades hold some value, they should constitute a small part of the overall assessment. Most feedback should emphasize enhancing learning and provide multiple opportunities for student success. Assessment plays a crucial role in final grades, but they shouldn't rely solely on traditional exams that reward correct answers. A grading structure that recognizes participation and effort is more effective in motivating students to improve (Swinton, 2010).

Instead, our goal in this work is to equip teachers with effective strategies for gathering evidence from students to make informed instructional decisions, fostering a supportive learning environment viewed through a lens of fluidity. We want professionals, students, and parents to see grades as fluid rather than final.

Imagine the norm being parents asking students not, "What grade did you get?" but rather, "What feedback did you receive, and what's your next step?" This would be a shift that encourages a mindset of ongoing learning where grades serve as road markers on a journey focused on progress and improvement. We desire to enable teachers to determine their impact through grading and feedback, moving away from traditional practices lacking research backing (Guskey, 2019).

Our aim is ultimately to create schools and classrooms where grades communicate goals and expectations and serve as milestones on a journey, not destinations—where learning is viewed with a sense of fluidity rather than one of finality.

REFLECT AND CONSIDER

Right now, how do you, your colleagues, your students, and other stakeholders view grades in your school . . . with more finality or more fluidity? •

_____
_____
_____
_____
_____

Throughout the text, we will focus intently on the importance of clarity as a driver of assessment, feedback, and grading actions in all schools and classrooms. Each chapter will have some specific objectives, but the following are overarching success criteria that readers should be able to accomplish throughout the text.

SUCCESS CRITERIA

As a reader, after reading the subsequent chapters, I will be able to

1. Recognize certain commonly held beliefs about grading actions that may inhibit both student achievement and student assessment capabilities

2. Recognize the paradox between research and evidence related to grading and feedback versus the day-to-day actions of classroom teachers

3. Understand the six traits of a visible learner who drives their own learning and how grading and feedback actions can promote these traits in students or undermine them

4. Understand the alignment between research and evidence to grading practices at the school and classroom level

(Continued)

(Continued)

5. Determine grading and feedback actions that are simply incongruent with Visible Learning and research and need to be abandoned
6. Determine specific grading and feedback actions that can replace those that are incongruent with research that are still easily adaptable and implementable into classroom practice
7. Recognize how to monitor the impact of grading and feedback actions on both student learning and achievement as well as desired behaviors ●

NOTES

CHAPTER 2

Developing Visible Learners Through Grading

"The purpose of education is to turn mirrors into windows."

—Sydney J. Harris

John Hattie and his Visible Learning research provides educators with actions, ways of thinking, approaches, and strategies that have been shown to have the best chance to increase the probability of learning (see Figure 2.1). Hattie recently updated his findings with the release of *Visible Learning: The Sequel,* (Routledge, 2023). This sequel includes his updated findings from over 60 years of meta-analyses on actions that have had the greatest impact on student achievement.

FIGURE 2.1: DISTRIBUTION OF EFFECTS

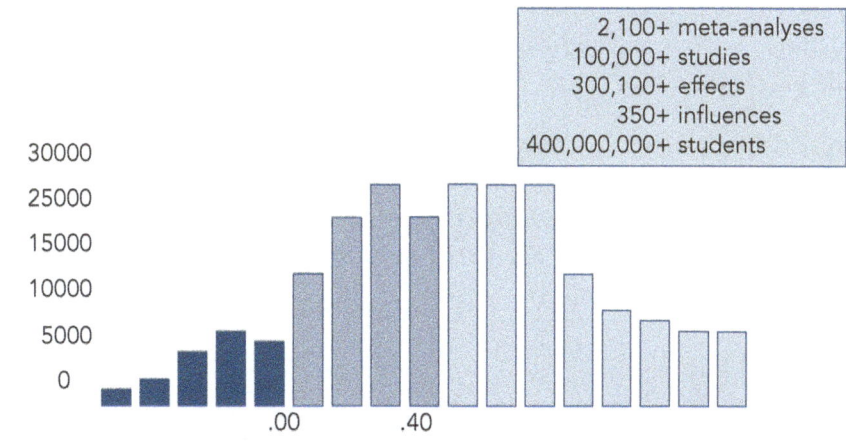

SOURCE: Adapted from Hattie (2023).

Unlike other research studies, Hattie conducted meta-analyses of meta-analyses (large-scale studies of large-scale studies) that have included more than 100,000 studies and involved 400,000,000 students. We will highlight many of Hattie's research influences throughout this book as a guide for determining grading and feedback actions that will likely have the best opportunity to increase learning.

SUCCESS CRITERIA

As a reader, after reading this chapter I will be able to

1. Understand the traits of visible learners, students who drive their own learning
2. Recognize how certain grading actions can promote or deter these traits from being developed in students •

Developing Great *Learners*

How are your teaching actions and approaches developing your students as good learners? That is a paramount question every teacher and collaborative team or professional learning community (PLC) should be asking on a regular basis. Nurturing students as learners should not be secondary to teaching content. We do espouse teachers develop students as *good* learners *through* the content and subject matter they teach—it's not an either or, rather *and*. All of Professor John Hattie's work and research focuses on determining which instructional actions and approaches best impact student learning and developing the best learners we can in our classrooms.

Figure 2.2 lists traits of visible learners. It is easily argued that all teachers would desire these traits and behaviors to be cultivated in each and every one of our own students. A visible learner, or what we now call students that drive *their* learning, can answer these three questions anytime they are learning anything:

1) What am I learning?

2) How will I know when I have learned (it)?

3) What are my next learning steps?

We must keep these questions at the forefront anytime we are assessing where students are in their learning. The first two questions relate specifically to the level of teacher clarity present in classrooms: Have students been made aware of the learning goals as well as the criteria needed to demonstrate when they reach those goals?

FIGURE 2.2: CHARACTERISTICS OF VISIBLE LEARNERS

- **KNOW** their current level of understanding
- **KNOW** where they are going and are confident to take on the challenge
- **SELECT** tools to guide their learning
- **SEEK** feedback and recognize that errors are opportunities to learn
- **MONITOR** their progress and adjust their learning
- **RECOGNIZE** their learning and teach others

SOURCE: Adapted from Frey et al. (2018)

It's that third question (*What are my next learning steps?*) that is sometimes the hardest to unpack. Teachers will be able to develop visible learners by being *visible teachers*. Dave, a former biology teacher, realized his main goal was not to teach science but rather to help students become better learners through life science.

Teachers use various tests and assessments to provide feedback and calculate grades. To enhance learning, students must answer the critical question, "What do I do next?" This requires them to interpret their scores, which can unlock significant potential for both their learning and motivation.

Visible learners do not settle for simply being assessed and graded. They are engaged drivers of their own learning who derive value and pride from their own progress. Helping your learners understand and unlock their potential does not just impact school achievement goals—it reminds us all what it really means to learn. Students who can answer these questions are more likely to see the big picture of assessment and how it fits into the grand equation of learning. They look past their score and are interested in how they learn and what they need to learn. They will then and only then view learning with *fluidity not finality!*

Overview of the Six Traits of a *Visible Learner*, Who Drives Their Own Learning

1. **Know their current level of understanding:** Based on clearly defined and shared criteria, students can tell you what they have mastered, what they are working on, and where they are going next in their learning.

2. **Know where they are going and are confident to take on the challenge:** Learning is challenging, but helping students understand their

progress and prepare for the next challenge fosters their motivation and engagement. Teachers must identify the right tasks to appropriately challenge and engage each student to embrace the will, skill, and thrill of learning.

3. **Select tools to guide their learning:** Not every problem needs a hammer, and not every screw needs the same screwdriver. Helping students know which tool to apply in different situations and which one is best for them is key. Learners need to know when to use different strategies and even more need to know what to do . . . *when they don't know what to do!*

4. **Seek feedback and recognize that errors are opportunities to learn:** Feedback is one of the most powerful influences and allows students to see error as a normal and expected path to success. When students pursue feedback to grow and develop, they become their own teacher. The key is to ensure your feedback is heard, understood, and actionable by your students.

5. **Monitor their progress and adjust their learning:** Learning is about progress, and accelerated progress leads to higher achievement. It focuses on the journey and the question, "Where to next?" Feedback from assessments is a key teaching tool. Students must learn to adjust their learning, so grading and actions should reflect their progress.

6. **Recognize their learning and teach others:** When students are taught to interpret results related to their learning, they become more adept at knowing what they have learned and how to impart that learning to others. Students teaching and teachers learning is when *Visible Learning* is truly taking place.

Teachers Are the Catalysts

John Hattie summarized all of his research and influences as to what factors most impact student learning. First and foremost are the students themselves (see Figure 2.3). This is not a surprise. Students are in most control of their learning, but after that, teachers are the *second* most important variable in student learning, more important than students' home environment, peers, the school structure, or the leadership within the school combined. We hope this finding is not a shock to anyone and reinforces just how important individual classroom teachers are to the achievement and learning of their students. Thus, when it comes to the topic of grading, it is incumbent upon all educators to create meaningful learning opportunities so students can be assessed and given feedback that moves their learning forward while cultivating the traits we wish them to have.

The primary goal in every classroom is to create great learners who drive their own learning. Classroom teachers have the greatest impact and influence over the learning of their students so developing learners should not pause just because we have to administer grades.

Teachers must embrace the notion that grades are a reflection of both student learning and the *quality of their instruction*. Grades communicate to students where they

FIGURE 2.3: INFLUENCES ON STUDENT LEARNING

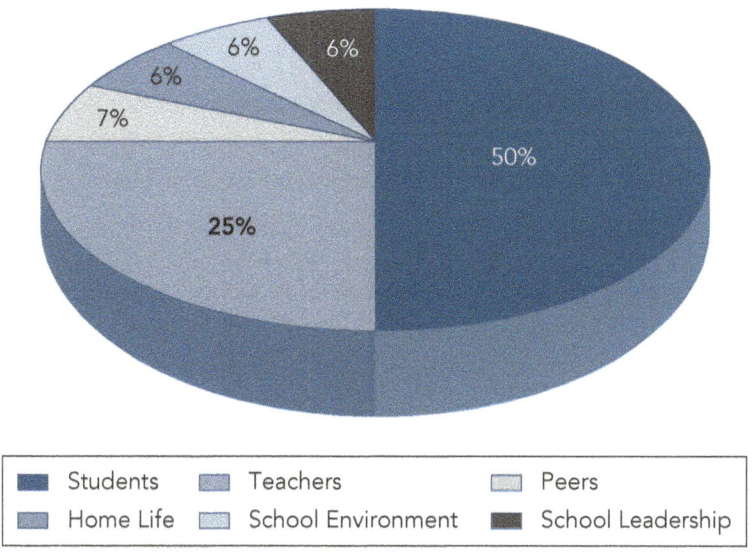

SOURCE: Reprinted from Visible Learning Foundation Day Resource Guide.

are in the learning process as much for the student as for the teacher. Assessments and grades are feedback to teachers about the three *visible learner questions*:

- What did I teach well, and what do I need to cover again?
- Who did I teach well, and to whom do I need to return?
- How great was the growth shown, and what and who needs acceleration?

G.R.A.D.E.S

So how do we grade *visible learners*? We do so in the same way we try to develop them with other classroom actions. We have created the acronym G.R.A.D.E.S (see Figure 2.4) to describe grading and feedback actions that align to and support the

FIGURE 2.4: G.R.A.D.E.S.

- **G**auge their current level of understanding
- **R**eadiness to know where they are going and are confident to take on the challenge
- **A**dapt tools to guide their learning
- **D**etermine feedback, and recognize that errors are opportunities to learn
- **E**valuate their progress, and adjust their learning
- (Be) **S**uccessful in recognizing their learning and teach others

six traits of students who drive their own learning. In the subsequent chapters, we will address how to support students and cultivate each one of these traits through specific grading practices and actions. We will examine grading from the perspective of the student and teacher to adapt current practices that match what we desire from all our students.

Grades should indicate a student's current performance, but visible learners should always be asking, "Now what?" This critical question of "Where do I go next?" drives teachers to support students in understanding their learning progress and future steps. When grades are aligned with feedback, they empower both teachers and students to identify areas for deeper learning. Students should receive guidance on how to advance their learning, using grades as communication on "now what" and as a foundation for future growth. Grades should be accompanied by timely, specific feedback that clarifies next steps, transforming grades from final judgments into opportunities for continuous learning and growth. Table 2.1 provides some reflection and considerations.

TABLE 2.1: GRADING REFLECTIONS AND QUESTIONS TO CONSIDER WHEN DEVELOPING VISIBLE LEARNERS

TRAIT	REFLECTION QUESTION	GRADING AND FEEDBACK CONSIDERATIONS
Gauge their current level of understanding	How do you elicit student learning evidence before instruction to determine the best starting point?	All learners must understand their starting point and their destination. Teacher clarity is paramount; they must clearly define expected learning goals and how students will demonstrate them. Teachers should ensure that tasks and assignments provide evidence and feedback for both teachers and students to guide their next learning steps.
Readiness to know where they are going and are confident to take on the challenge	How do you determine if students are being properly challenged?	Hattie emphasizes that tasks should be neither too difficult nor too dull. If learning tasks don't let students apply skills and surpass basic understanding, they are seen as separate tasks to finish. When tasks are perceived as isolated, students focus on completion without considering the learning involved or the next steps.

TRAIT	REFLECTION QUESTION	GRADING AND FEEDBACK CONSIDERATIONS
Adapt tools to guide their learning	How are students provided opportunities to determine the path they use for learning or to demonstrate mastery?	We must avoid early grading as it diverts students' attention from the strategies needed for further learning (Kluger & DeNisi, 1996). Harsh grading early on can leave students feeling defeated, leading them to give up or avoid challenges. Conversely, if students receive high grades too early, they may become overconfident, resistant to new challenges, and avoid taking risks.
Determine feedback, and recognize that errors are opportunities to learn	What do you do to promote a classroom culture that views error as a *necessary path to learning and growth*?	We can't encourage students to see errors as learning opportunities while counting every mistake in the gradebook. To view learning as a process and embrace error, we must foster a supportive classroom environment. Consistently awarding perfect scores is considered educational malpractice. However, careless mistakes or those from a lack of effort should be penalized, with the penalty proportionate to the time and effort needed for correction.
Evaluate their progress, and adjust their learning	How often do your students self-assess to determine their next learning steps against success criteria?	Students need to develop strong self-regulation to identify their best strategies and learning choices. We can't foster ownership of learning if we limit students to only one path or option.
(Be) Successful in recognizing their learning, and teach others	What do you currently do to promote ways for students to teach others?	Students should see themselves and their peers as learning drivers. Teaching others enhances learning. Nuthall (2007) found that 80 percent of peer feedback is often incorrect due to misunderstandings of success criteria. Students need opportunities to focus their collaboration on teaching and learning from one another.

CHAPTER REFLECTION

1. How are traits of effective learners viewed as something to develop in the students in your school?

2. How are grades and grading practices currently viewed in your school or district? Are they viewed as a method to drive academic success and increase the traits we hope to cultivate in our students?

3. How do your students interpret their grades, and how informative are these interpretations for them?

NOTES

CHAPTER 3

Challenges to Grading Visible Learners

"Grades don't measure tenacity, courage, leadership, guts or whatever you want to call it. Teachers or any other persons in a position of authority should never tell anybody they will not succeed because they did not get all A's in school."

—Thomas J. Stanley

In Chapter 2, we outlined six traits of students who drive their learning, or visible learners. We would be hard pressed to find any teacher who would not want to develop or augment those traits in all of their students. Feedback is a key aspect of doing so.

Grades do have the potential to provide *meaningful*, accurate, and honest feedback to students, parents, and subsequent teachers. So why often don't they?

 **SUCCESS CRITERIA**

As a reader, after reading this chapter, I will be able to

1. Consider traditional grading actions that impede learning
2. Recognize some commonly held beliefs impede effective classroom practice

(Continued)

(Continued)

3. Use the task/assignment grading matrix to create more impactful practice and reinforcement experiences for students

4. Determine ways to combat student disengagement

5. Plan in advance for cognitive barriers to engagement ●

Teachers often struggle with grading, but this challenge does not diminish their dedication, expertise, or passion for their profession. Effective grading as a course is rarely included in teacher preparation programs as well as professional learning settings (Feldman, 2018). We have been in countless situations as professional developers working with schools and districts on topics related to clarity, feedback, assessment, and so on, during which the leader said, "please don't get them going about grades or grading actions." Which made us wonder: Why do we sometimes avoid talking about grading? Grading practice conversations often evoke strong emotions. All of us have had grading done to us and often use our experience as students as a basis for our beliefs and actions. Balancing emotion and reason is challenging, yet there are concrete reasons for teachers and school leaders to recognize why grades often fail to hold true meaning and hinder the development of students who drive their learning. As teachers, professional learning community (PLC) teams, school, and district leaders work to cultivate students who take charge of their learning—using grading as a catalyst rather than a barrier—they must consider these five potential roadblocks to grades being meaningful in promoting students as great learners.

> Five Grading Roadblocks to Developing Great Learners
>
> 1. Traditions trumping evidence
> 2. Commonly held beliefs (specifically related to student assignments)
> 3. Absence of collaboration around grading
> 4. Focusing too much on processes students follow
> 5. Not considering students' cognitive engagement

1. Traditions Trumping Evidence

Schools are steeped in traditions, from athletic rivalries and pep rallies to year-end celebrations. These events foster pride among students, faculty, the community, and alumni, and their significance is unquestionable. However, there are other longstanding practices that affect teaching and learning, often upheld by parents and stakeholders who have preconceived notions of how schools should function. These traditions are carried out often without consideration of examining their impact, simply because they were part of our own educational experiences. We must pause and ask ourselves, "Does this truly make sense? Does it align with our goals? Is there perhaps a different approach to consider?"

Averaging Grades

Mathematicians quip: *The mean is the least reliable number of a data set.* This is because it takes into account every data point. Outliers in any distribution can be skewed to affect the mean, one single outlier can drag the mean down or up. We believe we must *eradicate the average* in grading. Grades are feedback, so the notion that a complete mathematical average of student performance, taking into account every success, mistake, aspect of proficiency, shortcoming, opportunity to practice and improve, where they succeeded or failed, would be boilerplated into an accurate depiction of where that student's learning is *today* needs to be abolished.

To view learning with fluidity and not finality calls for all educators to focus on the progress of learning and accuracy of where the learner is *now . . . today*. If a student struggled previously and is now starting to improve and succeed, that is also a sign of good teaching and should be accurately depicted in the form of a grade.

> *As the World Health Organization did for smallpox in the 1970s, teachers and leaders could do as much for grading health by finally eradicating once and for all the practice of averaging students' final grades. Many researchers have discarded the idea that averaging should play any role in determining grades (Guskey & Bailey, 2001, 2009; Kirschenbaum et al., 1971; Marzano, 2006; O'Connor, 2009, 2010; Reeves, 2004, 2009, 2011; Wormeli, 2006).*
>
> (Nagel, 2015)

One SINGLE Letter Grade

This is a difficult one because life is full of examples where the traditional concept of letter grades (A-B-C-D-F) is used. NFL teams are *graded* on how well experts feel they did drafting players in the spring prior to the upcoming season (Kiper, 2023). Restaurants in certain states by law have to post the grade they received from their last health inspection. We use these letters because they have internal meaning to almost everyone. After cooking a meal for our kids we will sometimes ask them, "how did Dad do?" Invariably, they will use a letter grade that is based on several things: the taste, the amount, the presentation, and so on. To determine what we should do differently, we should ask, "So how was the taste? More salt, less salt? What could have been better about the presentation?" The point is a letter grade gets us in the ballpark but doesn't tell us what seat we are in. Specificity is needed to determine next learning steps. If a singular grade encompasses many different elements, it's virtually impossible to do that. Standard-based reporting does provide the level of specificity we are talking about, and we certainly encourage the practice. We believe schools can overcome this hurdle even if they do not shift into a full standards-based reporting system or report card. We address this concept in Chapters 7, 8, and 9.

Homework as a Determining Factor for Grades

Homework is practice. Homework started early in the 20th century when compulsory education became the standard in the form of seatwork. After school each day, students tended to fields and did needed chores at home. Seatwork was for students to deliberately practice math facts, writing, and so on to solidify foundational skills. Once fewer students were going home to work in the fields, seatwork was sent home. At some point, seat work and the deliberate practice element of homework morphed and became whatever work wasn't completed in school. If students have to teach themselves what to do it is no longer practice. Hattie (2009) found high school teachers were most likely to assign homework for students to actually learn the subject matter themselves rather than from the teacher delivering instruction. We will address this in detail in Chapter 10.

Valedictorian

Many high schools honor their top graduates with esteem and recognize them in front of the entire community at commencement. These students *earn* the privilege of giving a speech in front of their classmates, family, and relatives by having the highest grade point average (GPA) of their graduating class. The ranking system for valedictorian in most high schools is typically based on a mathematical formula that is inherently vague and ambiguous. This frequently promotes unnecessary competition between students (Nagel, 2015). Guskey (2015b) noted that, "this pits each student against all others for one singular distinction, and this often results in aggressive and sometimes bitter competition among high achieving students to be that top-ranked individual" (p. 65). Could this be a tradition that needs to be re-examined? Having one student recognized above all others by $1\frac{1}{1000}$ of decimal point difference in their GPA over four years is rarely congruent with anything that will happen again in life. Some colleges share how students in a particular program compare to their peers in a specific tract or program, but few have a race in which only one student wins. Most colleges and universities recognize levels of high achievement such as magna cum laude, summa cum laude, and cum laude. In addition, the National Association for College Admission Counseling as recently as 2019 noted that class rank is the ninth factor out of 15 considered when determining college admissions (https://www.nacacnet.org/factors-in-college-admission/). Many school districts have moved to a model of graduates with honors, high honors, and so on (Nagel, 2015). We acknowledge the notion not recognizing the graduate with the highest GPA might be viewed as intriguing to some and blasphemous to others, but it is something to consider.

2. Commonly Held Beliefs

There are many commonly held beliefs educators have about grading. These beliefs drive actions and sometimes prevent us from making adjustments in practice. We want to clarify that this is not a critique of any teacher's belief about the desire to have freedom and autonomy in their classroom. Often these beliefs are innate and go unspoken. We list several commonly held beliefs that relate to the ideas and concepts we are addressing in each chapter starting with Chapter 7. We call them commonly held beliefs because they aren't necessarily 100 percent true or false, right or wrong. For each commonly held belief about grading, we will offer a counterpoint, trying to make a case that the some commonly held belief does not support developing visible learners and students who drive their learning through grading. We acknowledge that not all commonly held beliefs we will speak to are held as true by all educators. Very often, commonly held beliefs come from our experience as students or anecdotes. Debates about the impact of any classroom or school strategy or action need not be anecdote free, but they should not be anecdote exclusive.

EXAMPLE INCLUDED IN CHAPTER 11

COMMONLY HELD BELIEF	COUNTERPOINT
Giving kids more work when they are done accelerates and challenges them.	Teachers' desire to push students to achieve more and accelerate their learning is well warranted. The challenge arises when we blanketly assume that students *should always* accept additional work/rigorous challenges simply because they have met learning targets *ahead of schedule or ahead of their peers.*

Assignments Matter

There are many commonly held beliefs related to how teachers assign work, tasks, and so on to students and how they are used in grading and feedback. Here are some examples:

- All students need to have the same assignments to be fair related to grading.

- All assignments students complete increase their learning.

- Any assignment that students do poorly on, and decreases their grade, also decreases their level of learning.
- Any assignment students complete that increases their grade also increases their learning.

None of these belief statements is completely true or false nor do they originate from a place of ill will or desire not to perform well as a teacher. Our counterpoint to all four is that *all assignments are not equal in their value, worth, or most importantly impact on learning*. Because of that we have developed the assignment grading matrix shown in Figure 3.1.

FIGURE 3.1: ASSIGNMENT/TASK GRADING MATRIX

	Improvement of Learning and Achievement →
Improvement of Grade ↑	**Coasting**: Tasks lead to grade increases with no increase in learning or achievement | **Thriving**: Increase of learning and achievement along with increase in academic grade
	Losing: Grade either stays same or decreases with no increase in learning/achievement | **Developing**: Learning/achievement increases without an increase in academic grade

To use the matrix, educators can place any task into one of the four quadrants. For the purpose of understanding, we will consider any task to be an assignment, homework, test, quiz, performance, classwork, lab, or so on. The more a task improves student grades the higher you would move up the vertical axis, while the more a task improves *student learning and achievement*, the more you would move to the right on the horizontal axis.

Losing: Tasks that do not increase student grades or learning. We call them *losing* because they lead to a loss of time, opportunity to increase learning of important concepts and skills, ability to impact student confidence and success, and so on. These are tasks students do poorly on or perhaps don't even complete, and thus, there is a decrease in their overall grade; but, if they did complete them it would not have made a difference in their learning anyway.

Coasting: Tasks that increase a student's grade but do not increase their learning. These are sometimes considered fluff assignments or ones specifically administered to students to simply complete. We call these tasks coasting because they provide little to no cognitive challenge and at times are administered for students to complete *just to raise their overall grade or average*. Stronger students like these because they do not have to face a challenge to complete them. These can lead to students shying away from more difficult tasks in fear of missing out on easy points or grades. Coasting tasks that are not completed and thus lower the grade would then fall into the losing category.

Developing: These are tasks that provide quality inferences for both students and teachers as to where students need to go next in their learning. Students may struggle with these tasks, but they foster learning and growth. These *developing* tasks help teachers determine if students have any underlying prior knowledge gaps before they move on to deeper understanding of the curriculum. Eradicating the average in grading allows teachers the ability to administer tasks to students they don't do well on but learn from them without fear of not being able to improve their grade in the future.

Thriving: These tasks increase learning and achievement as well as the student's grade. We call these thriving because that is what they do for students and teachers. Students and teachers reaching this quadrant on a regular basis with their tasks likely will need to engage in some that fall into the developing quadrant but avoid the other two. There must be clarity of what learning is to be demonstrated from all tasks to reach this quadrant consistently.

This quadrant concept for thriving is not Pollyanna. It is hard work that requires teachers to work in tandem with students on understanding what learning is expected to come from any task students engage in.

We have provided some example descriptions of tasks, not an exhaustive list, that would fall into each quadrant in Figure 3.2.

FIGURE 3.2: EXAMPLE TASKS

CATEGORY	EXAMPLE TASK, ASSIGNMENTS, ASSESSMENT

Losing	• Busywork assignments
	• Worksheets/projects:
	   ○ With repetitive or simplistic questions, little to no challenge or critical thinking
	   ○ Requiring only memorization of facts/dates without context or deeper understanding of the subject matter.
	   ○ Involving regurgitating information from a text or lecture without analysis or synthesizing the material.
	• Homework for sake of homework—not to reinforce learning or provide additional practice
	• Tests/quizzes on trivial or minutiae details
	• Group projects where workload is totally unevenly distributed

(Continued)

(Continued)

CATEGORY	EXAMPLE TASK, ASSIGNMENTS, ASSESSMENT
Coasting	- Busy sheets—worksheets that provide little to no challenge or connection to existing work or curricula - Easy, low-effort assignments that inflate grades without challenge to students to deepen understanding or skills - Extra credit assignments based on completion, not requiring demonstration of understanding or mastery of material - Assignments heavily reliant on rote memorization or regurgitation of facts - Bonus points for tasks unrelated to course material or learning objectives, such as bringing in tissues or donating school supplies - Points given for attendance, participation, or completion of nonacademic tasks - Assignments that heavily weigh factors unrelated to academic performance, such as neatness of handwriting or adherence to arbitrary formatting guidelines. - Grade inflation through curving or adjusting scores due to peers scoring lower on task
Developing	- Powersheets—note taking, graphic organizers, data collection and inference making, and so on - Group projects where communication and collaboration were challenging, leading to a lower grade but a deeper understanding of teamwork and problem-solving - Presentations where a student struggles with speaking expectations but develops skills in organization, research, and preparation. - Training tasks that focused on prerequisite skills (See Chapter 9) - Written tasks for which student receives lower grade but improves writing skills and critical thinking
Thriving	- Differentiated tasks focused on individual students' strengths and learning styles, allowing demonstration mastery in various ways (Missing Essential Assignments Extended Chance, MEAECs) (See Chapter 10) - Project-based assessments that require application of knowledge and skills to real-world scenarios, fostering critical thinking and problem-solving abilities - Collaborative projects promoting teamwork and communication skills—also deepening students' understanding of the subject matter - Socratic seminars/class discussions encouraging active participation, critical analysis, and deeper engagement with the material (See Chapter 11) - Performance tasks allowing students to showcase understanding through creative means, such as presentations, skits, or multimedia projects - Peer-reviewed assignments and peer grading tasks providing students with feedback from peers, promoting self-reflection and continuous improvement (See Chapter 10)

3. Absence of Collaboration Around Grading

Teacher collaboration, often in the format of PLCs, rarely involves discussions related to grading practices and actions. Teacher collaboration must focus on educators monitoring the impact of all adult actions on learning to develop a culture of collaborative expertise. Expecting collaboration around the impact of grades should be a nonstarter. We are not talking about a group of teachers sitting around grading papers together. And besides, if you see teachers grading papers together that is not a PLC meeting. *We usually call that a staff meeting!* Collaboration around grading involves teachers examining tasks and assignments for rigor level *before* they are administered to students, collaborative scoring and analysis of student work, determining actions to prevent unnecessary failure, and so on. We will speak of the critical need for structured collaborative dialogue and discussion around grading actions as core practice in all schools in Chapter 4.

4. (Too Much) of a Focus on Grading Process Criteria

Grades should serve as formative feedback throughout the learning journey, not just at the end of a lesson or semester. Reporting separate grades for product, process, and progress increases their meaning (Guskey, 2015b). Teachers should consider all three factors when providing feedback and determining grades.

We must be cautious not to base grades too heavily on student processes such as following directions or completing mundane or frivolous tasks. These inflate grades without having to embrace more challenging and complex tasks (coasting). Moreover, here is where teachers overreward students who are pleasant and compliant in class, completing assignments neatly and on time but not necessarily producing work that meets required criteria. A survey by MacMillan (2001) found that effort and participation are often the main factors influencing grades among 1,483 teachers in Grades 6-12. Thus, using an assignment and task grading matrix can help educators evaluate assignments before grading or assigning them to students.

Process Focus Leads to Giving Students Undesired Carrots

Finally, grades are often erroneously considered to be a carrot intended to motivate students. We hear often that what used to motivate students, poor grades for example, doesn't anymore. Well, we believe it never really did, it's simply a game that fewer students in 2025 are interested in playing. In classrooms where grades are over emphasized, students tend to attribute performance to ability rather than effort (Ames, 1992). Therefore, using grades as a carrot to promote effort may defeat the purpose (Guskey & Brookhart, 2019)!

5. Not Considering Cognitive Engagement

There are many challenges to increasing the learning of students in any classroom. One that is often mentioned is getting students to be more engaged. To help students become drivers of their learning, we must empower them to self-assess their cognitive engagement levels. In 2022, researcher and author Amy Berry developed a continuum of engagement that provides a framework for teachers to help students become aware of their engagement levels during learning experiences (see Figure 3.3). Berry's model provides guidance and a tangible construct for students to be able to self-assess their current levels of cognitive engagement based on their behaviors. Her model provides teachers guidance with a concrete tool to use with their students to help *them* (the students) be more aware of where their current level of engagement is any time they are learning.

FIGURE 3.3: CONTINUUM OF ENGAGEMENT

A Continuum of Engagement					
Active ←——————— Passive ———————→ Driving					
DISRUPTING	AVOIDING	WITHDRAWING	PARTICIPATING	INVESTING	DRIVING
Distracting others Disrupting the learning	Looking for ways to avoid Off-task behaviour	Being distracted Physically separated from the group	Paying attention Doing work Responding to questions	Asking questions Valuing the learning	Setting goals Seeking feedback Self-assessment
DISENGAGEMENT			ENGAGEMENT		

SOURCE: Adapted from Berry (2020).

Lack of Engagement Antecedents

Helping students determine their level of engagement is of little use unless teachers have an understanding why students disengage. Research by Chew and Cerbin (2020) shows that different cognitive barriers to learning require specific teacher approaches (see Table 3.1). Without addressing these, students face poor grades and ongoing learning challenges.

TABLE 3.1: NINE BARRIERS TO COGNITIVE ENGAGEMENT

COGNITIVE BARRIER	REASONING
Student mental mindset	The student may be disruptive due to insecurity or past failures, feeling that they lack the ability to learn the topic or see its purpose.
Metacognition and self-regulation	Some students may be overconfident, leading to a lack of focus, or they may not realize their inattentiveness is causing them to fall behind. They might also struggle with skills to refocus on the task.
Student fear and mistrust	The student may have a strained teacher relationship or long-standing negative school experiences, possibly due to bullying or trauma.
Insufficient prior knowledge	These students lack the prerequisite knowledge and skills to master the learning for that day's work.
Misconceptions	A student might persist in misconceptions, such as adding denominators when adding fractions, even when presented with evidence to the contrary.
Ineffective learning strategies	They use ineffective strategies and get frustrated with their lack of progress, lacking alternative approaches when their current ones fail.
Transfer of learning	They struggle to apply learned skills to new problems, feeling defeated and giving up when their practice differs slightly from the model.
Constraints of selective attention	They either believe they can multitask or focus on irrelevant classroom activities.
Constraints of mental effort and working memory	The task may be too complex or require too much working memory, causing students to get lost.

CHAPTER REFLECTION

1. Which of the five factors reducing the meaningfulness of grades resonates most with you?
2. How can you plan for engaging students by navigating the barriers to engagement?
3. What actions might you take in your school or classroom to minimize the challenges to developing visible learners through grading?

NOTES

CHAPTER 4

Core Grading Actions and the SI²TE Model

"In all things you do, above all else, be true to your core!" What makes and fulfills you, done well, will sustain you.

—Anonymous

In Chapter 2, we examined the six traits or dispositions of visible learners who drive their own learning. The work of all educators must be on developing learners in all classrooms not as a replacement of a focus on achievement but as the catalyst that drives student achievement. This requires specific actions and practices that are consistent and routine in every classroom. In our profession, we often hear the phrase "we need to focus on best practices," and we do not disagree. We espouse that for something to *be a best practice* it absolutely must be a *sustainable practice*.

To embark on a path or continue efforts to develop visible learners and improve the quality of feedback through grading practices, we believe there are four core actions all schools can and should implement: teacher collaboration, clarity of scoring, collaborative scoring/feedback of student work, and multiple opportunities for success through stipulated second chances. This is a slight adaptation from what Dave spoke to in 2015 in his book, *Effective Grading Practices for Secondary Teachers*. It is erroneous to presume that simply creating new grading policies, regardless of how firmly mandated, will lead to fidelity of classroom practices. Subject matter and grade level context will impact how specific classroom grading practices are implemented (Nagel, 2015, p. 84).

SUCCESS CRITERIA

As a reader, after reading this chapter, I will be able to

1. Describe four core actions that schools can implement to drive impact into grading and feedback actions

    a. Teacher collaboration

    b. Clarity of scoring

    c. Collaborative scoring/analysis of student work

    d. Stipulated second chances

2. Utilize the SI²TE Framework as a guide for adjusting current grading and feedback actions to support student learning

Core Practice 1: Teacher Collaboration

The notion, however, that all teachers are created equally is pure fiction. There is a great deal of variability among teachers in terms of the effect and impact they have on student learning. Teachers see classrooms, interpret actions, and critique themselves very differently. This variability is well known and extremely valuable but rarely discussed, and it is why we need to strive for collaborative expertise (Hattie, 2015).

Schools can increase the effectiveness of adult actions while monitoring their impact through collaborative settings. Discussing collaborative interpretations of evidence of impact of teaching actions on student learning is the main purpose of having professional learning communities (PLCs). In Hattie and Zierer's (2018) *10 Mindframes for Visible Learning*, they call for teachers to *collaborate with my peers and my students about my conception of progress and my impact*. The message is clear: Teachers need to hear second opinions related to their impact on student learning. For our work, this is another way to frame it: How do we collectively interpret the grades and make decisions about where to next? Too often, grading decisions take place in isolation. Worse yet, they happen in large-group settings without protocols needed for effective discussions that can then build trust where teachers share interpretations of evidence, engage in collegial inquiry, and share views of progress and potential next steps for *where to next* for individual students or classes.

VIGNETTES

The ninth-tenth grade English Language Arts (ELA) PLC team at Everywhere High School has been charged with determining some common grading actions and practices that they can work into their PLC learning cycles. The team comprises seven teachers, five of whom have been together for the past four years. From observations, they have functioned fairly well together. They regularly work together to analyze common standards for units, determine success criteria, develop common assessments, analyze student data, and work to determine common strategies. Conversations related to any common grading practices have rarely taken place, however. During their first PLC meeting of the school year, the team leader, Joan, opened the meeting by reminding everyone that grading practices would need to be a commonly revisited topic.

Joan: Well guys, we have our roles established, norms agreed upon, and our curriculum maps are fairly set as to when units will begin and common assessments will be administered. We need to talk about how we will look at our grading actions. What are some topics around grading we might want to address?

Mike: I don't really think we need to spend much time here, I mean we all are going to grade the best way we see fit for our classes. I know some of you guys accept late work, but from my experience, that doesn't do anything to get these kids ready for the real world. I mean if you miss deadlines at your job you will get fired! . . . It's as simple as that!

Besty: Well I don't know if I agree. Last year when I implemented amnesty days, my kids who were behind got caught up, and I was pleased with how much more engaged they were.

Dave: I agree. I mean we aren't saying we won't have deadlines, but the goal is to get them to the finish line, and sometimes that means we throw a lifeline.

Susan: I'm with Mike. I am starting a no late homework policy in my class, and any missed assignments are zeros—no exception.

Joan: (Trying to rein the group back in). Well, I think we will need to talk about this point for sure, but there are many other things related to grading that are more pertinent. I was thinking we could make a list . . . (Gets cut off)

(Continued)

(Continued)

Phil: I'm sorry guys—I will follow the curriculum like we have talked about and make sure we all agree on scoring the common assessments, but my day-to-day teaching and grading isn't really something I think any of you would be able to follow. I give points for how kids participate in discussions, if kids are helpful and cooperative, and I add additional points if they are on the cusp of a grade, and I am pretty sure no one else does that.

Susan: Yeah, and I allow open books for chapter tests, and I know Dave you said you would never do that, which is fine. Joan, you use success criteria as the basis for how and what you grade, I am not even sure what that is. I think we need to realize we are all somewhat different here, and the kids figure it out.

Group Talking Over Each Other: *"I do that sometimes." "Me too . . . " Oh my gosh, I never would do that, how does that teach them to study?' "Etc . . . Etc . . . "*

Arguing began to ensue over a couple of comments made, and eventually Joan told the group they would just table the conversation for another meeting.

. . . It never happened! ●

That is not the type of collaboration that will help teams create and implement effective grading practices, let alone ones that are designed in a way to support our students becoming the best possible learners.

PLC Dialogue Around Grading to Impact Beliefs

Collaborative teams or PLCs need to develop shared meaning from what we collectively see in student results through dialogue. The word *dialogue* comes from Greek: "dia-logos" to see through to something's meaning. To engage in dialogue is to intentionally seek to understand by listening deeply, inquiring, and advocating in order to uncover meanings and reveal assumptions.

PLC dialogue must focus on improving student performance, not simply reporting on status. Effective PLCs have the capacity to promote and sustain the learning of all professionals in the school community and thus impact student learning through adjustments in practice. It is, however, important to keep in mind that "enhancing pupil learning is the foremost concern" (Bolam et al., 2005, p. 145). Interpretations about grading practices and approaches must be an expected aspect of PLC discussions and dialogue. PLCs must dedicate specific time for collaborative concentration on monitoring how grading and feedback practices are impacting student achievement as well as how they support developing visible learners.

Effective collaboration around grading as a core practice can begin to challenge certain commonly held beliefs teachers have about grading practices (see Chapter 2 and Figure 4.1). Hattie (2012) notes that how we think as educators underpins our every action and decision. Teachers have "theories of practice" for how to accomplish all they have to do within an established set of resources, such as the available time they have. Hattie also points out that, over time, as experience in teaching increases, teachers' theories of practice (e.g., grading practices) become more pervasive in teachers' minds as the best way to do things (Nagel, 2015).

FIGURE 4.1: GRADING COLLABORATION TOPICS AND EXAMPLES

TOPICS	DESCRIPTION/EXAMPLE	HOW OFTEN
Start of School Year Grading Decisions	Teachers determine when unit/common assessments will be administered and what will be included. If appropriate, predetermine buffer days between units designated for reteaching. Collaborate on common elements of syllabi. Plan for stipulated second chances (multiple opportunities for success).	Prior to start of school year See Appendix 1 for Self-Reflection Tool
Assignment/Task Analysis	Teams regularly analyze assignments and tasks for alignment to standards and success criteria as well as for agreement on rigor level.	2–3 times per 9 weeks See Chapter 4
Agreement on *Truthful* Grading–Means Grades Represent Accurate Levels of Achievement	Teams determine what evidence of learning related to standards, specific success criteria, and so on should be demonstrated to receive specific grades. *For example, for students to receive at least a B or proficiency, they would have to demonstrate knowledge of X concepts and demonstration of X skills.*	Prior to start of school year/quarter/trimester/unit See Chapter 8 and Appendix 2 for examples of parameters to drive grading policy

(Continued)

(Continued)

TOPICS	DESCRIPTION/EXAMPLE	HOW OFTEN
Monitoring Impact	Teachers determine expected outcomes for both student academic learning as well as student behavioral elements aligned to adult actions.	Regularly
Failure Prevention, Multi-Tiered System of Support	Teachers provide early intervention for students demonstrating signs of academic concerns. Focus time on both identifying reasons for student failure as well as adult actions to address and prevent future failures. Team determines actions to address both *affective factors* (not working, lack of engagement, etc.) as well as instructional adjustments needed for skill gaps. Team commits to specific actions as well as dates to monitor results.	Emphasis early in the school year/semester and revisited at least monthly, several times per quarter. See Appendix 3, 4, & 5 for Failure Prevention Tools
Collaborative Scoring/ Analysis of Student Work	See Core Practice 3	Regularly throughout the year, (2–3 times per semester). See Chapter 10.

Example: Expected Grading Collaboration

Fontana Unified School District in California has written into its board-approved secondary grading policy recommendations an expectation for teacher collaboration. Using the district's existing PLC model, several parameters are explicit in the policy as recommended practices:

Professional Learning Communities (PLCs) will have agreed upon like weighting and like categories for determining student grades.

- Teachers shall allow students to retake assessments within the guidelines established by the PLC.
- Clear learning objectives and grading criteria shall be explicitly communicated to students and parents at the beginning of the course. Course-alike teachers at each site will have similar syllabus expectations.

- PLCs should work together to create a common syllabus that includes assignments that are both formative and summative.

To see their Grading Policy in full, scan the QR Code here:

 To read a QR code, you must have a smartphone or tablet with a camera. We recommend that you download a QR code reader app that is made specifically for your phone or tablet brand.

https://bit.ly/4dURdbs

 **REFLECT AND CONSIDER**

What is the level (quantity/quality) of collaboration around grading in your school(s)?

_____
_____
_____
_____
_____

Core Practice 2: Clarity of Scoring

Grading requires clarity for accurate interpretation. Guskey (2021) stresses that grading must start with its purpose, specifying what, why, and how student work is scored. A shared understanding of grading purposes ensures clarity. Communicating grading criteria helps students grasp expectations and the evaluation process. This transparency reduces ambiguity and allows students to concentrate on learning targets.

Clarity in scoring enhances feedback effectiveness, which is crucial for student growth by allowing them to identify strengths and areas for improvement. This enables teachers to provide specific guidance to help students overcome challenges and build on successes, illustrating the value of their work in relation to learning objectives. When grades accurately reflect student skills, they recognize the relevance of learning, fostering intrinsic motivation and a deeper appreciation for their growth efforts. Furthermore, clarity supports instructional planning and differentiation by helping teachers understand student performance against standards, allowing for personalized learning experiences. It also facilitates communication with stakeholders, like parents and administrators, providing a reliable measure of progress that informs decisions and policies. Collaborative meetings further enhance grading organization, ensuring effective assessment (Welsh & D'Agostino, 2009). Chapter 6 will go into clarity of scoring in more detail.

Core Practice 3: Collaborative Scoring and Feedback of Student Work

In *Classroom Grading and Assessment That Work,* Marzano (2006, p. 61) notes that when two teachers used a common scoring system for the same work, the reliability of the combined score was found to be as high as 0.82. Summative early research noted that inconsistency in teachers grades came from a variety of sources:

- Criteria for evaluating work
- Teacher severity or leniency
- Differences in tasks
- Teacher error

(Guskey & Brookhart, 2019)

Pauly (2009) defined *collaborative scoring* as "teachers gathering together to use a standards based rubric to score student work" (p. 14). Reliability in grading increases when teachers grade sets of student work samples anonymously and do so with the lens of tying grading and feedback to success criteria. This removes any preconceived personal beliefs or perceptions about individual student's ability during the scoring and grading process. Teachers have the ability to let their moral judgments influence the grades they assign (Zoeckler, 2005). What matters most then is how students and teachers react to the grades regarding what next steps in learning should or should not happen.

VIGNETTES

Weekly PLC meetings at Wonder Middle School had been focused on ensuring students receive quality feedback related to their learning and teachers made the best instructional decisions. Leadership provided time for teachers to meet with colleagues of like subject matter from their own and other grade levels.

For example, this past fall, the sixth, seventh, and eighth grade ELA teachers examined selected samples of anonymous student writing and talked about what they were seeing, how they would score the work consistently, and what feedback they would provide their learners. This drove deep discussions about their teaching practices and about the characteristics of developing quality writers who could own their next learning steps.

Through this intentional process, teachers developed a shared vocabulary for describing their teaching and feedback actions. This work directly informed their classroom practice.

During subsequent PLC meetings, teachers met in adjacent grade level groups—sixth-seventh and seventh-eighth to look at samples of student writing. Seventh grade teachers had an opportunity to see what their former students were now doing in eighth grade and the specific ways their writers had grown. This quasilongitudinal examination of their current students helped teachers identify patterns in writing development and actions that were having the greatest impact.

Individual samples of student work became places along the learning journey rather than the destination. Their actions affirm their beliefs in viewing learning with fluidity, not finality. ●

REFLECT AND CONSIDER

Developing visible learners through grading requires teachers and teams to consistently collaborate to examine student work aligned with teacher actions.

How often do your PLC teams use collaborative time to focus on grading and feedback actions? How often is student work collaboratively scored or collaboratively provided feedback? ●

_____

_____

_____

_____

Core Practice 4: Multiple Opportunities for Success Through Stipulated Second Chances

When students have opportunities to revise and improve work, they view trial and error as a way to learn from mistakes and are more likely to seek additional challenges and build resilience. Friedman (1998) mentions that many teachers "like to point out to students what they can learn from their mistakes" (p. 79). However, if teachers don't offer multiple opportunities for students to display proficiency, they are *not* allowing students to learn from their mistakes. When students develop proficiency over time they develop resilience, as well perseverance and persistence, or as Duckworth (2016) calls it, *grit!* This increases how they value and more effectively use teacher feedback. However, if students receive well thought out extensive ideas for how to improve their work or performance but there is no opportunity to actually use the information to improve or adjust their work, then they will consider them less and less useful over time.

The practice of providing multiple opportunities for students to revise and improve their work is so they *can improve their learning, not just improve their grade*. When student grades are determined and the feedback they are provided is based on students' true and *current* demonstration of proficiency, rather than by averaging each student's individual attempts, consistency of grades between teachers increases dramatically (Nagel, 2015).

Make-Up Testing Myths and Truths

Educators too often misconstrue multiple opportunities as meaning redundant test taking. Any quality assessment has three attributes: purpose, evidence, and the inferences we make from the results. First, teachers decide on the *purpose* of their assessment (what standard concept or skill is it assessing?). Then they determine how to make accurate inferences from the *evidence* students provide. If a student takes the exact same test over and over, and on the fifth try scores a passing or proficient grade, the teacher would not be sure the student hadn't simply memorized the answers.

The idea of make-up tests and redoing assignments does have tremendous potential for student motivation. A 2023 article in *Edweek* featured a study that surveyed over 1,000 students aged 13 to 19 about some of the best ideas to motivate them. The results were telling. The opportunity to redo assignments was the *most selected response*, with over 35 percent of students saying that would motivate them the most to do well in school (Prothero, 2023). For students to grow in their learning, they may need alternative assessment methods with multiple avenues to accurately assess their next learning step.

Stipulated Second Chances

Life is full of second (and third) chances, but they often come with stipulations. For example, teachers who do not pass their certification exam always have the chance to retake it—with the penalty of the cost of the test and additional time dedicated to studying for the next exam. They don't start lower on the pay scale when they are hired. Income tax extensions can be filed for a small fee. And let's face it, *people who pass the bar exam on the ninth try are still called attorneys (or some are simply called My Cousin Vinny!)* When any learner uses three to four attempts to reach mastery, what have they demonstrated? Here's what: *perseverance and persistence or grit, and using feedback to understand their next learning step—which they used to develop mastery.* Isn't this a trait we want to cultivate in our students?

Stipulated second chances offer students multiple opportunities to grow in their learning and develop skills of visible learners, while adding a layer of accountability for students to understand that in life there are second and often third or fourth chances, but they do come with an additional cost. Stipulated second chances also make teachers feel less concerned about allowing students additional attempts to reach learning goals, when they feel students may have thumbed their nose at them the first time. Many teachers have a strong desire, and rightly so, to ensure their academic teaching does not completely eliminate their ability to teach students some degree of responsibility and accountability (Nagel, 2015).

Real-life stipulated second chances often come with an additional cost. The currency students desire that teachers can barter for in exchange for providing them second chance stipulations to be able to make up work, retake tests, or show proficiency on the second or third or fourth attempt—is their precious time. When students lose the privilege of free time, teachers can focus on increasing their achievement and learning while still providing students with a dose of real-world experience for missing deadlines or failing to follow through on responsibilities. Stipulated second chances actually increase students' responsibility to learn without distorting the accuracy of academic grades, much more than not allowing a chance for completing work or tasks simply because a deadline was missed.

EXAMPLES OF STIPULATED SECOND CHANCES

- Teachers allow students to make up missing work before or after school (or during any designated free time)
- Requiring a written reflection by student for how they prepared for reassessment perhaps with parent signature

(Continued)

(Continued)

- Written work must include additional sources or citations
- Work must be ready for submission to a journal, school or local newspaper, or school board
- Students must share work with the class via presentation or some mode of technology
- Work time is provided for students to complete work, retake assessments, and so on before school, during lunch or recess, afterschool, or other times designated for students to have as free •

See Appendix 6 for sample Stipulated Second Chances Contract

REFLECT AND CONSIDER

What is the current reality related to allowing students to retake assessments/tasks? How could the concept of stipulated second chances be implemented into your school or classroom? •

_____
_____
_____
_____
_____

When schools, teams, and individual classroom teachers are considering grading actions and approaches to increase student academic performance as well as to cultivate the traits of visible learners, we propose utilizing the SI^{2}TE Model Framework (See Figure 4.2). This is an evolution of the model Dave developed and first showcased in 2015 for teachers and teams to consider when supporting struggling learners and preventing unnecessary failures (Nagel, 2015). Each element described in the following sections can be used to provide guidance for determining actions and strategies to develop students who are great learners. We will highlight specific school and classroom actions aligned to the model in subsequent chapters.

FIGURE 4.2: SUPPORTING VISIBLE LEARNERS

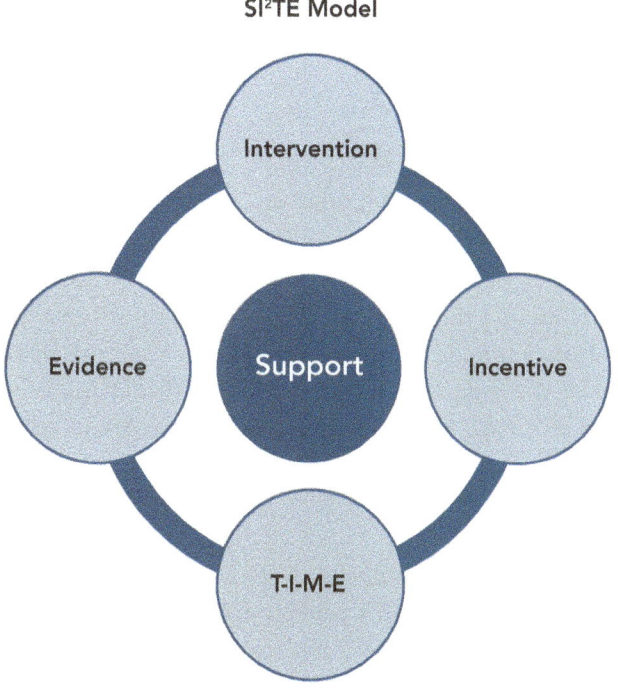

SOURCE: Reprinted from Nagel (2015).

Support Students in Feeling Safe to Take Risks and Overcome Challenges

The first element of SI²TE is support. Developing visible learners begins and ends with students understanding any current academic struggles are not permanent. When students do not feel a sense of support from adults, they develop learned helplessness and view academic adversity as permanent or beyond their control. Students who feel their teachers are a support network for them will exert higher levels of effort and engagement and are less likely to *even consider dropping out of school* (Yazzie-Mintz, 2010). In the recent Programme for International Student Assessment (PISA) studies across many countries, only 60% of students reported that, in most lessons, the teacher showed an interest in every student's learning or continued teaching until students understood the material (PISA, n.d.).

Students who struggle frequently have a history of academic failure, lacking both the necessary skills and resilience to persist through challenges. Those who experience repeated failures from middle school into high school often accept this as their norm, resulting in decreased effort and engagement. Teaching the skill of perseverance is crucial for developing the resilience needed for success in high school and beyond. Nan Henderson of Resiliency in Action emphasizes that "caring and support" are key to building student resilience (2013, p. 24). Moreover, grading practices must support students and convey that success through hard work is achievable, rather than inflating grades through easy assignments. Misrepresenting achievement levels by allowing students to pass without demonstrating mastery can hinder resilience development (Perkins-Gough, 2013). Raising grades without corresponding achievement fosters a culture of low expectations (Nagel, 2015).

Finally, it is just as critical for students who are strong academically to know they are supported in taking on new challenges in their learning. Often, these students fear any form of failure or lack of perfection and avoid taking risks if they will not be completely successful and thus threaten their self-image as a bright student! When students feel a sense of support, they are more likely to set goals that are challenging and to stretch their thinking. Students must not feel that taking risks in their learning will lead to detrimental effects in their grades. See example in Chapter 7.

(Early) Intervention

Dave's college professor from Butler University in Indianapolis, Dr. Steve Heck, often quipped, "Amateurs react and repair, professionals prepare and prevent." This is the essence of what early invention means. Teachers' best chance to prevent student failure is by intervening as soon as they see signs of it. Students' perception of being supported early is also critical as it relates to their motivation to learn. Betterhighschools.org notes that failure of one class is a "threshold" indicator, meaning that failing even one course places students past the onset of potentially dropping out. They recommend that teachers evaluate grades between twenty and thirty days after the start of the semester to look for signs that some students may need intervention (Hanover Research, 2013). See example in Chapter 11.

Increase Incentives (Not Consequences)

When teachers and PLC teams prioritize incentives over consequences in grading and feedback, they can reduce unnecessary failures and guide students toward better learning choices. Research indicates that incentivizing student input (efforts) rather than outputs (proficiency) effectively mitigates the negative impacts of failing grades (Allan & Fryer, 2011). The belief that low grades teach the importance of effort is unfounded; using grades to reward positive behavior or punish misconduct has not proven effective in enhancing student learning or promoting desired behaviors (McMillan et al., 2002). Moreover, there is no evidence that penalizing students with low grades increases effort (Guskey, 2009).

When we talk of incentives, we are not positioning it as simply extrinsic rewards for quality work turned in on time with a friendly disposition. Hattie and Donoghue (2016) label the "skill, will, and thrill" of learning as the core element of learning strategies to instill in all students. This involves helping ensure that students have the skills they need, the proper mindset to make sure learning happens, and the motivation to deepen their understanding *before a new lesson*. Deep motivation and approach (d = 0.58) occurs when students desire mastery or deeper understanding of what they are learning. This drives students to a higher degree of investment to have a fuller understanding overall of the topic (https://www.visiblelearningmetax.com/influences/view/deep_motivation_and_approach). Incentivizing students to show what they know with the *incentive or reward being* less necessitated work or more options for ownership in their next learning task will go much further in developing visible learners and less simply compliant ones. See example in Chapter 9.

T-I-M-E as the Variable (Learning Must Be the Constant)

Time is the one variable schools completely control when it comes to grading and feedback while keeping learning as the constant. This is a challenge teachers often face when attempting to ensure adequate coverage of curriculum targets for all students. We must focus on what *students are learning and the progress they are making toward curriculum targets* as opposed to the time frame allotted. Students behind in skill and knowledge will need additional time to learn prior to being evaluated by in the form of a grade. Teachers create unnecessary problems by not offering students additional time, as that can "motivate the student to do exactly the opposite behavior than intended" (O'Conner, 2017). If students feel additional time will not be provided or points will be deducted for lateness of work, many will cease attempting to complete it. Overly harsh grading or late penalties increase anxiety with older students; such penalties often create defiance to not do homework at all (Vatterott, 2009, p. 75). O'Connor (2009) quotes Joel Barkey, saying, "It is best to do it right and on time, but it is better to do it right and late than the reverse" (p. 100). See examples in Chapters 8 and 11.

Gather the Right Evidence

The final element of the SI²TE Model Framework is *evidence*. Teachers must use the best and most current evidence of learning and progress when grading their students, especially when the possibility of failure looms. Student failure dramatically decreases when teachers ensure students are working on the most important aspects of the curriculum and use the best evidence essential of content and skills (Nagel, 2015). (See Missing Essential Assignments Extended Chances [MEAECs] Chapter 10)

The less certain teachers are about a student's proficiency, the *more* assessment evidence they should collect and use (Marzano, 2006, p. 114). This may mean collecting *more* evidence on certain concepts and skill understanding for some students and not wasting time gathering evidence unrelated to lessons and units' academic focus. This is where the assignment-task grading matrix introduced in Chapter 3 can be helpful. This allows students to demonstrate evidence of the most important learning to prevent failure and build student resilience. See example in Chapter 7.

Each of these five elements of the SI²TE Model Framework can serve as a guide for classroom teachers and PLCs to use and consider when creating or adjusting grading and feedback actions to prevent student failure and cultivate the traits of visible learners. Finally, grading practices that fall under this framework should not diminish rigor or student accountability to complete necessary work. Instead, focus more on opportunities students can be offered to demonstrate academic success and develop traits that arm them to take on future challenges in their learning.

 **CHAPTER REFLECTION**

1. What opportunities are considered for improving grading actions when considering the four core grading actions to embed into all classrooms and schools:

    a. Teacher collaboration

    b. Clarity of scoring

    c. Collaborative scoring/analysis of student work

    d. Stipulated second chances

2. How could you use the SI²TE Model Framework as a guide for adjusting current grading and feedback actions to support student learning?

NOTES

CHAPTER 5

Mindframes and Beliefs Drive Actions to Impact Student Learning

"Student engagement is not always about hands-on actions; it is not about busy work. Intellectual involvement is the definition of true engagement."

(Danielson, 2007)

Effective teaching hinges on a deep understanding of how students learn, the diverse traits they bring to the learning environment, and the clarity with which teachers present information. Teachers who thoughtfully consider student learning processes recognize the importance of tailoring their instruction to meet varied learning needs and styles. By identifying and fostering positive student learning traits, educators can create a more engaging and supportive classroom atmosphere. For example, teacher clarity in communicating goals, relevance, and desired outcomes ensures that students can navigate their learning paths with confidence and purpose, ultimately enhancing their academic success and personal growth. In short, visible learners who drive their learning are developed by visible teachers.

SUCCESS CRITERIA

As a reader, after reading this chapter, I will be able to

1. Understand the connection of the 10 Mindframes for Visible Learning to the individual traits of developing visible learners.

Beliefs Drive Actions

Grading practices in schools are often the most misaligned and inconsistent strategies, varying widely from one classroom to another. To address this inconsistency, we must deliberately plan our approach from the beginning. Beliefs significantly influence what individuals' study and the methods they employ, particularly regarding the factors they deem relevant to their practice (Bandura & National Institute of Mental Health, 1986).

Visible learning means an enhanced role for teachers as they become evaluators of their own teaching. Mindframes allow teachers to better evaluate their impact on learning. "It is more about how they think about what they do that matters most, how they understand their impact, and their search for feedback" (Hattie, 2012). To enhance our approach to instructional design and the tasks we create for supporting learning, we must recognize the significance of assessing our impact and using grading as an effective communication tool. Beliefs are also the focus for instruction. Teaching has to do, in part at least, with the formation of beliefs, and that means that it has to do not simply with what we shall believe but with how we shall believe it. Teaching is an activity that has to do, among other things, with the modification and formation of belief systems (Green, 1971).

The research supporting these beliefs, including Hattie's mindframes, is dynamic, evolving from the original *Visible Learning* book in 2009, which featured over 800 meta-analyses, to *Visible Learning: The Sequel* (2023), encompassing more than 2,100 meta-analyses, enriching our understanding.

Ultimately, our perceptions about our work and beliefs regarding visible learning shape our effectiveness. The first mindframe, "I am an evaluator of my impact on student learning," serves as a foundation for the other nine (see Figure 5.1).

FIGURE 5.1: THE TEN MINDFRAMES FOR VISIBLE LEARNING

IMPACT	
1	I am an evaluator of my impact on student learning.
2	I see assessment as informing my impact and next steps.
3	I collaborate with my peers and my students about my conceptions.
CHANGE AND CHALLENGE	
4	I am a change agent and believe all students can improve.
5	I strive for challenge and not merely "doing your best."
LEARNING FOCUS	
6	I give and help students understand feedback, and I interpret and act on feedback given to me.
7	I engage as much in dialogue as monologue.
8	I explicitly inform students what successful impact looks from the outset.
9	I build relationships and trust so that learning can occur in a place where it is safe to make mistakes and learn from others.
10	I focus on learning and the language of learning.

Linking Desired Learner Traits to Mindframes

Great learners are not born; they are developed by visible teachers. Making teaching visible is an active process that begins with how educators think about their role and learning itself. As Hattie (2009) notes, one of the most significant influences on student achievement is how teachers approach learning and view their own role. The actions stemming from these beliefs shape the dispositions we seek in our students. The link between teacher mindset and student outcomes is crucial for promoting learning, achievement, and visible learner traits. Figure 5.2 highlights some examples of specific teacher mindframes that align with the development of traits of students who drive their learning. All of the mindframes support cultivating these traits. We will highlight key examples of where there are very strong connections. When educators adopt these mindframes, their students reap the greatest benefits.

FIGURE 5.2: ALIGNING MAINFRAMES TO VISIBLE LEARNER TRAIT

MINDFRAME	POWER IN DEVELOPING DESIRED LEARNER TRAIT
• I am an evaluator of my impact on student learning • I am a change agent and believe all students can improve.	When teachers assess their impact and believe in every student's potential, they foster a supportive environment. By customizing tasks and providing constructive feedback, they promote student awareness of progress, encouraging reflection and goal-setting for academic growth.
• I see assessment as informing my impact and next steps. • I strive for challenge and not merely "doing your best."	When teachers use assessment to evaluate their impact and plan next steps, they can better identify student strengths and areas for improvement. This focus shifts from mere effort to growth and mastery. By adopting this mindset, teachers help students recognize their progress and set clear, achievable goals. Consequently, students gain clarity on their learning path and, backed by their teachers' confidence, are more likely to develop the resilience needed to face new challenges. This approach empowers students to take ownership of their learning and pursue continuous improvement.
• I collaborate with my peers and my students about my conceptions. • I engage as much in dialogue as monologue.	Teacher collaboration with peers and students fosters a dynamic learning environment that deepens understanding. With peers, it escalates the potential of developing collaborative expertise. With students, it conveys a desire to help students become the drivers of their learning. Through dialogue, teachers share strategies, clarify concepts, and promote active student participation, as well as listen to how learners feel actions and approaches are supporting their learning journey. This exchange keeps instruction innovative and equips students with the skills to take charge of their learning.
• I build relationships and trust so that learning can occur in a place where it is safe to make mistakes and learn from others. • I give and help students understand feedback, and I interpret and act on feedback given to me.	Frey et al. (2018) argue that feedback is "the most underutilized approach we have as teachers." By fostering a supportive environment where mistakes are safe, teachers build trust and encourage risk-taking. Consistent constructive feedback helps students view errors as learning opportunities and encourages mutual respect. When teachers model openness to feedback, students are likely to adopt the same mindset, using feedback actively to enhance their learning and promote continuous improvement.
• I explicitly inform students what successful impact looks from the outset. • I focus on learning and the language of learning.	Teachers assist learners in assessing their progress by providing clear success criteria and ongoing self-assessment guidance. They explicitly define success and offer detailed feedback, helping students understand their goals and necessary steps. By emphasizing learning language, teachers clarify objectives and encourage self-reflection, enabling students to identify areas for improvement and adapt their strategies. As students recognize their learning, they gain confidence and can teach others, fostering collaboration. Ultimately, by guiding self-evaluation and establishing a clear success framework, teachers empower students to become self-directed learners committed to continuous growth and peer contribution.

CHAPTER REFLECTION

1. In what ways have your beliefs impacted your classroom actions and approaches?
2. How do you feel beliefs help determine how we view traditional grading actions?

NOTES

NOTES

CHAPTER 6

Bringing Clarity to Grading

"The art of teaching is clarity and the art of learning is to listen."

—Vandana Shiva

Clarity of Grading Scoring Guide

Teacher clarity is crucial for aligning classroom practices, including assessment, feedback, and grading. Without clarity, students cannot take charge of their learning. Grades must be seen as essential feedback for gauging learning progress. Clarity narrows the gap between students' perceptions of their learning, their engagement, and their final evaluations. As Guskey and Brookhart emphasize, effective evaluation hinges on clarity; poorly measured performance leads to flawed decisions (Guskey, 2024).

Fendick (1990) and Titsworth et al. (2015) both note that teacher clarity is more than the presence of learning intentions and success criteria. They describe teacher clarity as having four distinct components: organization, explanation, examples and guided practice, and assessment of student learning.

To completely implement a model of teacher clarity, we call for the inclusion of *clarity of scoring*. We have developed the Clarity of Grading Scoring Guide (CGSG; Figure 6.1) to assist teachers and PLC teams in designing tasks that foster mastery of key learning standards. It provides a framework for scoring and grading tasks that demonstrate student learning, enabling teachers to qualitatively communicate students' achievements and progress toward mastery. The guide also offers examples to navigate scoring considerations for different levels of cognitive challenge.

FIGURE 6.1: HOLISTIC CLARITY OF GRADING SCORING GUIDE (CGSG)

Mindframes for Learning: Which Is a Focus for This Unit/Lesson	*Visible Learner Trait to Be Developed*
I am an evaluator of my impact on student learning. I see assessment as informing my impact and next steps. I collaborate with my peers and my students about my conceptions. I am a change agent and believe all students can improve. I strive for challenge and not merely "doing your best." I give and help students understand feedback, and I interpret and act on feedback given to me. I engage as much in dialogue as monologue. I explicitly inform students what successful impact looks from the outset. I build relationships and trust so that learning can occur in a place where it is safe to make mistakes and learn from others. I focus on learning and the language of learning.	**Gauge** current level of understanding **Readiness** to know where they are going and confident to take on the challenge **Adapt** tools to guide their learning **Determine** feedback and recognize that errors are opportunities to learn **Evaluate** their progress and adjust their learning **Successful** in recognizing their learning and teach others

	GENERATIVE LEARNING EXPERIENCES	WEIGHTED SCORING
SURFACE	**SOLO**-*The learner identifies isolated pieces of information and is unaware of any connections.* **Concept Introduction With Vocabulary Recall (Retrieving)** Help students begin to recognize and retrieve key vocabulary or basic facts related to a new concept by engaging in structured recall exercises **Guided Retrieval With Fill-in-the-Blank (Recalling)** Help students recall basic facts or steps related to a new concept through structured fill-in-the-blank exercises that prompt memory retrieval	0.5X
	SOLO-*The learner recognizes several information points related to a topic but lacks a clear understanding of how they are interconnected.* **Fact Sorting Activity (Identifying Isolated Information)** Help students recognize and process multiple pieces of information related to a new concept by sorting and categorizing them **Concept Web Development (Recognizing Isolated Information)** Guide students in identifying and processing multiple components of a larger topic through the creation of a concept web	X

	PRECIPICE OF COGNITIVE CHALLENGE	
DEEP	**SOLO**-*The learner comprehends the relationships and connections between related concepts and ideas.* **Linking Experience: Concept Map Creation** Students will create a concept map to visually represent the connections between related ideas and concepts within a unit. **Analyzing Experience: Case Study Comparison** Students will analyze two case studies to identify similarities and differences, fostering deeper understanding of the relationships between concepts. **Applying Experience: Real-World Problem Solving** Students will apply their knowledge of related concepts to devise solutions for real-world problems, showcasing their understanding of the material.	1.5X
TRANSFER	**SOLO**-*The learner can extend and apply their knowledge to different contexts.* **Analogical Reasoning** Have students compare new concepts or problems to those they've previously encountered by identifying underlying patterns or principles. **Simulations and Role-Playing** Use simulations or role-playing scenarios that mimic real-world situations, requiring students to apply their knowledge in a practical context. **Case-Based Learning** Present students with diverse case studies that require them to apply their learning to solve new, complex problems. **Project-Based Learning (PBL)** Assign long-term, interdisciplinary projects that require students to apply their skills across various subject areas.	2X

 ## SUCCESS CRITERIA

As a reader, after reading this chapter, I will be able to

1. Determine the importance of clarity related to instruction, assessment, and grading actions

2. Understand the critical role generative learning experiences play in applying a score to student work

3. Determine how my PLC team could use the Clarity of Grading Scoring Guide

Benefits of using the CGSG include, but are not limited to the following:

- Increased effective teacher collaboration related to grading
    - A more robust focus of essential learning evidence from students versus collecting work from students to input in the gradebook
    - Increased aspects of collaborative scoring
- Promoting a focus on a specific visible learner trait to be developed through instructional assessment actions
- Determination of which mindframe(s) for learning teachers or teams are attempting to live out through their actions
- Elimination of busy or irrelevant work that provides a less-is-more approach by designing generative learning experiences supporting the most important skills and concepts
- Accurately weighing evidence by focusing on key elements to formally score related to the cognitive challenge or rigor
- Eradication of the averaging of grades
- A greater alignment between classroom grades and those of standardized tests

How Students Learn

At each learning phase—surface, deep, and transfer—we must align experiences with students' developmental stages. Surface learning introduces new concepts and skills, forming a foundation for deeper understanding. Students need ample practice at this stage to reinforce their knowledge. Deep learning builds on surface knowledge, fostering greater insights and requiring more time within this *optimal zone*. Finally, transfer learning occurs as students apply their solidified knowledge to new contexts and engage in metacognition.

Link to SOLO Taxonomy

As learning progresses, it becomes more complex. As teachers determine the appropriate level of experiences for where their students are in the instructional process, we've incorporated this concept into our CGSG. The SOLO (Structure of the Observed Learning Outcome) framework classifies learning outcomes by complexity (see Figure 6.2). Students move from understanding single elements (unistructural), to multiple unconnected parts (multistructural), to integrating these into a cohesive whole (relational), and finally extending this understanding to new situations (extended abstract).

Biggs (2014) emphasizes constructive alignment, starting with desired outcomes and aligning teaching and assessment to these. The verbs in outcome statements guide the learning activities needed, such as "apply" or "explain." Learning is built on student actions, not teacher actions, and assessment should measure how well students achieve the intended outcomes. SOLO helps map understanding levels into learning outcomes and creates assessment rubrics. Consistent scoring and grading are essential for providing students with clear feedback on their learning. See Chapter 7 for a specific example.

Figure 6.1 presents a holistic version of the CGSG, incorporating essential elements for grading that empower students to view learning as a fluid process rather than a final destination. In the following sections, we will detail each aspect of the instrument. Subsequent chapters will showcase specific examples of teachers and PLC teams across all grade levels using the guide to enhance their grading and feedback practices.

Mindframes for Learning

In Chapter 5, we discussed how the mindframes and beliefs we bring to the classroom drive our everyday actions and approaches. It would be difficult to impossible to live out all ten mindframes on a daily basis. That is not how they were designed or developed, nor would that be an expectation of any of us. We are encouraging the mindframes to be front and center of our thinking, planning, designing, and execution of our instruction, assessment, feedback, and last, but should never be viewed least, grading actions.

Visible Learner Trait to Be Developed

While designing tasks and learning experiences, teachers and teams should consider the visible learner trait they are attempting to cultivate with their students. This helps them identify specific adult actions that empower students to drive their learning from this experience and assessment. While obviously there is some overlap at times of these traits, they are unique in their own right. By having clarity of what disposition(s) we are trying to nurture and bring out in our students through the current content or curriculum we are teaching, we become more adept in determining the best actions to do so.

Designing Generative Learning Experiences

When planning instructional units, teachers must design evidence collection methods to demonstrate student learning at various levels. This planning should align with

Power or Priority Standards, ensuring that high-leverage skills and concepts guide instruction and determine grading weight. Educators must organize big ideas across the phases of learning—surface, deep, and transfer—while creating opportunities for students to practice what they learn. Dunlosky et al. (2013) emphasizes that schools often prioritize content over teaching effective learning strategies and evidence generation. Therefore, instruction should focus on generative learning experiences, allowing students to demonstrate their understanding through creation.

To empower students in driving their learning, they need opportunities to practice and generate their own knowledge. Grounded in cognitive science, generative learning encourages students to actively create knowledge by linking new information to their existing understanding (Almarode et al., 2021). This engagement leads to a deeper grasp of material, improved knowledge retention, and enhanced critical thinking and problem-solving skills. The essence of this approach is the "generation" process, where learners actively interpret and organize content rather than passively absorbing it.

Teachers face the challenge of determining next steps for all students based on their mastery levels. Elementary teachers may need to assess twenty-five students across various subjects, while secondary teachers may have over 150 students in one or two subjects. Supporting struggling students is critical; the slowest learners typically require five times more time to reach mastery than the fastest (Bloom, 1984). The CGSG provides examples for each learning phase—surface, deep, and transfer—to promote evidence generation and inform student learning.

Making Quality Inferences From Eliciting the Best Evidence

Quality teaching hinges on making well-founded inferences based on evidence gathered through classroom decisions. Teachers continuously face choices regarding readings, discussion groups, homework assignments, and assessment tools. They must thoughtfully design tasks, select media for presentations, plan pedagogies that leverage those tasks, and determine task complexity—all while anticipating ways to assess student learning (Sullivan et al., 2015). It is crucial to elicit the best evidence, rather than leaving it to chance.

For instance, just as a doctor asks you to fast before testing cholesterol to obtain accurate evidence for treatment, educators must strive to gather the best insights into student learning. Teachers and PLC teams should focus on making accurate estimates of student progress in relation to their goals and the complexity of assigned tasks. According to Hattie (2023), teacher estimates of achievement ($d = 1.46$) reflect how well teachers understand their students' learning relative to set objectives.

When teachers provide accurate estimates, they can make informed decisions about future activities, necessary challenges, questioning strategies, and student groupings. The more effectively tasks and experiences elicit strong evidence for inference making related to priority standards, the better equipped teachers will be to plan the next steps in learning.

The CGSG empowers teachers and PLCs to analyze planning phases to identify generative learning experiences that yield the best evidence for informed decision-making. It's not merely the validity and reliability of the assessment tools and tasks, but rather it is the ability to make sound inferences from the evidence gathered from those assessments (Popham, 2008). This reflective approach is essential for effective task design.

Weighted Scoring

The three models for task design are shown in Figure 6.3. All include some form of progression and scaffolding to empower teachers to determine where and when to increase the level of rigor while maintaining the key engagement elements of a task. Rigor in a task is not a single entity, it is not just the difficulty or just the complexity. Comparatively it includes cognition, strategy, and engaging qualities as intentional components of the design of the task (Antonetti & Stice, 2018).

FIGURE 6.2: THE SOLO TAXONOMY WITH SAMPLE VERBS INDICATING LEVELS OF UNDERSTANDING

Competence				
			Examine	Devise
			Utilize	Produce
			Debate	Postulate
		Merge	Evaluate/contrast	Contemplate
		Detail	Assess	Speculate
	Recognize	Count	Clarify → Reason	Theorize
	Label	Execute	Connect	
Fail	Adhere to basic	Sequential tasks	Defend	
Inept	protocol	Itemize		
Misses crux				
Incompetence	One relevant aspect	Several relevant independent aspects	Integrated into a structure	Generalized to new domain
Prestructural	**Unistructural**	**Multistructural**	**Relational**	**Extended Abstract**

SOURCE: Adapted from Biggs & Collins (1982).

FIGURE 6.3: RESEARCH EVIDENCE CALLING FOR TASK DESIGN CONSIDERATIONS

RESEARCHERS/ AUTHORS/SOURCE	NAME OR TITLE	INTENT OF USE AND APPLICATION	OBJECTIVES/BENEFITS
Biggs & Collis (1982)	SOLO Taxonomy	To describe levels of increasing complexity of student learning.	1. To provide a measure of cognitive learning outcomes or understanding of thinking 2. Assists educators in determining the intellectual level at which individual students can work and develop clear objectives in their framework
Antonetti & Stice (2018)	The Powerful Task Rubric for Designing Student Work	That design of task and actual implementation of task become visible to teachers, professional learning communities, and administrators	1. Learners experience the progression of a series of content tasks so as cognition deepens, engagement and strategy increase. 2. Teachers analyze the relationships between (and interdependence of) the three design components of a task.
Guskey et al. (2024)	The Table of Specifications	Empower educators to answer two essential questions when designing instruction: What do I want students to learn? (i.e., content) What do I want students to do? (i.e., performance)	1. Bring precision to teaching (lower and higher level learning skills) 2. Link instructional activities with learning targets (broad versus narrow standards) 3. Link texts and materials with learning targets 4. Align classroom assessments with learning targets

In applying the CGSG in practice, the sample experiences provided for each phase of learning serve as a planning tool for teachers and PLCs in designing their tasks. As the level of rigor increases moving down the template, the corresponding *weight of score* (WS), or value, placed on that learning experience increases. We have provided a generic example of a possible application of points, marks, or level earned for the corresponding experiences as 0.5X, X, 1.5X, and 2X as a guide. We will demonstrate with examples from teachers and teacher teams how they incorporate weighted scoring, regardless of the grading system they are using: traditional points or marks, standards based with criteria, or so on. As generative learning experiences become more rigorous and cognitively challenging, they support teachers and PLCs in creating and developing scalable tasks that assess students' mastery and guide their next learning steps. Consequently, these tasks carry greater significance in the learning process.

Rigor and Complexity as the Guide

We must dispel the belief that any grade or evaluation of student learning can be 100 percent accurate. Instead, we can enhance how we gather and examine evidence that contributes to the feedback students receive, focusing more on task complexity than mere completion.

Key to effective grading is acknowledging that not all tasks are created equal, especially regarding their rigor and complexity. The CGSG introduces the Precipice of Cognitive Challenge, highlighting tasks that demand higher-order thinking and skills of application and transfer, which are more rigorous than those requiring only comprehension. This aligns with Webb's Depth of Knowledge Level Three, where students apply strategic thinking to explore multifaceted questions and problems.

When designing tasks, those with increased rigor should carry greater weight in scoring, as they provide better evidence of students' deeper understanding of concepts. Weighted scoring reflects task complexity and allows for a nuanced evaluation of student performance. Assigning varying importance to assessments based on the evidence they yield empowers teachers and students to make stronger inferences about next steps in learning.

Additionally, incentivizing students to engage with more challenging tasks is crucial. Lang (2007) emphasized that proper incentives can encourage students to pursue advanced courses like advanced placement (AP) and International Baccalaureate (IB). Without these incentives, many may avoid challenges, leading to an inaccurate representation of their true capabilities. Additionally, Cognard (1996) found that schools that weighted grades for rigor shared a commitment to clearly defining excellence, reinforcing the value of challenging assignments.

Better Alignment Between Classroom Grades and Standardized Assessments

Research shows that grades lack consistency and reliability as measures of student performance. Stanford University researchers attribute many college students' struggles to the disconnect between high school coursework and standardized tests, which fail to align with college expectations (Cavanagh, 2003). Additionally, a growing mismatch exists between student grades and scores on standardized tests like the SAT and ACT (Najarro, 2024b). Discrepancies also arise when comparing grades to scores on exams aligned with K-12 coursework, including state tests and Advanced Placement assessments—students sometimes receive lower grades than their exam scores (Najarro, 2024a). Using the CGSG to weigh relevant skills and concepts according to priority standards can better align school report card grades with state and standardized assessments.

CGSG—A Strong Counselor, Not Jailor

The CGSG should serve as a guiding principle rather than a rigid rule, allowing for individualized evaluations to meet students' unique needs and educational settings. Through incorporating a thoughtful and adaptable approach to weighted scoring of graded work, educators can create a fair and supportive learning environment that promotes student growth and development as visible learners, similar to the evaluation process in Olympic events like diving and figure skating, where the degree of difficulty influences the final score.

Summary Benefit for Teachers: For teachers, clear grading criteria serve as a guiding principle for designing instruction. When teachers define what is important to grade and how they will score, they can better align their teaching strategies and activities with these priorities. This alignment ensures that instructional time is used efficiently, focusing on the most essential skills and knowledge students need to master and allowing them to create assessments that accurately measure student understanding and progress.

Summary Benefit for Students: For students, this transparency in grading fosters fairness and consistency. Students can trust that their work will be assessed based on clearly defined standards and the level of challenge they take on rather than subjective judgment. This trust is crucial in maintaining positive teacher-student relationships as well as to encourage students to take risks in their learning. When students perceive grading as fair, they are more likely to engage actively in their learning and use constructive feedback to move their learning forward. This trust also minimizes disputes over grades, as students and parents can see that assessments are based on objective criteria and scored accordingly and accurately.

 **VIGNETTES**

Throughout the remainder of the text, we will follow the journey of Wonder School District. A hypothetical but not fictitious K-12 system whose vision is to create an environment where teacher actions in every classroom are focused on developing great learners through the content or grade level they are teaching, while strongly emphasizing that learning is an ongoing journey, not a destination.

We will begin at Wonder Middle School where the eighth grade PLC team is meeting. They are determining the purpose of grading and striving to achieve deeper levels of clarity of scoring for tasks they will administer this fall.

PLC Lead: "Alright everyone, welcome. Today we're going to revisit our collective approaches to grading and look to create deeper levels of clarity of scoring across all subjects. Let's start by discussing the purpose of grading. What do we believe grading should accomplish?"

Math Teacher: "I think grading should accurately reflect students' understanding of the material and their progress toward meeting learning objectives."

English Teacher: "I agree. Grading should also provide feedback to students on their strengths and areas for improvement so they can adjust their learning strategies accordingly."

Science Teacher: "Absolutely. How we grade should help motivate students to engage with us and the material, not discourage them from taking risks or making errors. Grades should support students to strive for improvement, rather than just focusing on earning a certain grade."

Social Studies Teacher: "I think another important aspect is fairness. Grading should be fair and consistent across all students, regardless of their background or circumstances. We need to make sure we aren't inflating grades and allowing students who may struggle to coast with assignments that do not challenge them but would increase their grades."

PLC Lead: "Great points, everyone. Now, let's talk about how we can achieve clarity of scoring. How can we ensure that our grading criteria are clear and transparent to both students and parents?"

Math Teacher: "One idea is to clearly define our grading criteria and communicate them to students at the beginning of each unit or grading period."

English Teacher: "We could also provide examples of different levels of performance for each criterion based on the cognitive challenge within the tasks or assignments we will administer, so students know what is expected of them and what to expect in terms of difficulty on tasks."

Science Teacher: "I think it's important to use consistent language and terminology in our grading rubrics, so students understand exactly what each criteria means."

(Continued)

(Continued)

Social Studies Teacher:	"And we should be open to student questions and feedback about the grading criteria, so they feel empowered to advocate for themselves if they have concerns."
PLC Lead:	"Excellent suggestions, everyone. Let's compile all of these ideas into a set of grading guidelines that we can use consistently across all subjects. This will ensure that our grading is purposeful, fair, and transparent, ultimately benefiting our students' learning and growth. Maybe we can develop a tool or instrument we can all use. Let's plan to draft one next time we are together." ●

CHAPTER REFLECTION

1. When considering that not all tasks are created equal, and not all concepts or skills have equal impact on learning, how will your grading practices evolve?
2. How will you ensure you gather evidence rather than collect grades? ●

NOTES

Part II

Classroom and PLC Actions to Develop Each of the 6 Traits of a Visible Learner Through Grading

Each one of the next six chapters will address a specific trait of a visible learner who drives their learning with specific examples of classroom and school grading actions teachers and professional learning community (PLC) teams can take to develop them.

CHAPTER 7

Great Learners Gauge Their Current Level of Understanding

"It's a lack of clarity that creates chaos and frustration. Those emotions are poison to any living goal."

—Steve Maraboli

 **VIGNETTES**

Joe Smith, a dedicated seventh-grade social studies teacher at Anywhere Middle School, focuses on developing essential skills in his students. With ten years of experience, he fosters engagement through structured routines. Joe guides students in constructing evidence-based arguments but sometimes overemphasizes process adherence, risking grade deductions for noncompliance. Recently, he challenged his students to write an argumentative essay on the pros and cons of social media.

Joe scored three tasks related to this project:

1. Graphic Organizer
2. Essay
3. Presentation

(Continued)

(Continued)

He provided students with the following criteria to consider when submitting their work:

Graphic Organizer:

- Complete (neat)
- Organized ideas
- Cleary states side of argument you are on and possible counterpoints

Essay:

- Three paragraphs
- Neat (few grammar errors)
- States argument and reasons for taking that side

Presentation:

- Eight slides (one intro, one conclusion)
- All slides have at least one visual image and effect
- Makes solid eye contact during presentation to class
- Uses proper voice inflection
- Five to seven minutes in length

As usual, students were actively engaged, and most students completed tasks on time. Grades were based on each task weighing equally at 33.3 percent, ranging from 97 percent to 44 percent for those who completed all tasks. Joe grouped students by ability, planning to focus on reteaching students who struggled while challenging ones who excelled on the task.

Joe was surprised, if not shocked, to find students who he was fairly confident were more than adept at developing and defending an argument were in the group he identified as needing intense support and vice versa for some who really struggled in doing so.

He asked students to identify their next steps for making and defending an argument as an exit ticket, promoting ownership of their learning and revealing their perceived improvement needs. He was surprised by their responses, summarized below:

- Complete my graphic organizer
- Be more organized

- Have pictures on slides
- Fix spelling mistakes
- Use more slides
- Be clearer when talking

Several students who truly struggled and received low (below passing scores) stated that they didn't know how to get started. Joe was frustrated that few of the student responses for their learning step had anything to do with making a solid argument or defending it with evidence and data. ●

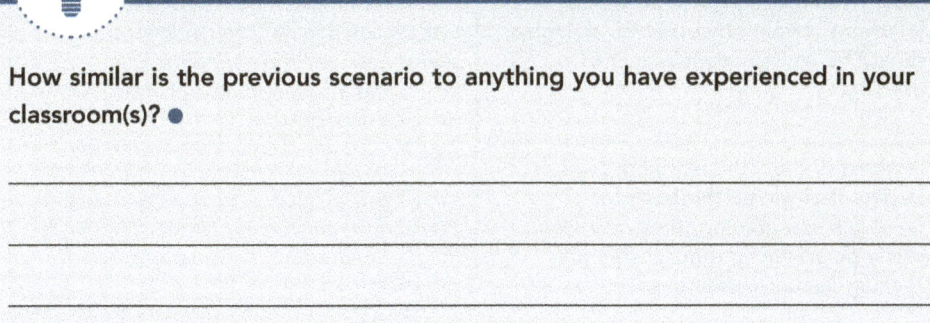

REFLECT AND CONSIDER

How similar is the previous scenario to anything you have experienced in your classroom(s)? ●

_____
_____
_____
_____
_____

Commonly Held Grading Beliefs

In the following chapters, we will examine common beliefs about grading and feedback discussed in Chapter 3 concerning barriers to developing visible learners. Hattie (2012) highlights that as we gain teaching experience, our theories of practice can solidify and may require disruption to explore alternatives. Many grading practices stem from our own school experiences and often prioritize grades over genuine learning. We will reassess certain grading beliefs, recognizing that our beliefs influence actions that can enhance or hinder student achievement (Hattie, 2012, p. 159).

SUCCESS CRITERIA

As a reader, after reading this chapter, I will be able to

1. Provide feedback to students that empowers them to gauge their level of understanding

2. Provide clarity in my instruction, the assessments I design, and the grades I assign

3. Understand that there are multiple levels of clarity (academic skills as well as behavioral dispositions) to consider related to feedback and grades •

COMMONLY HELD BELIEFS	COUNTERPOINT
Simply completing work, including following certain processes for doing so, should be an important aspect of grading.	Completion-based grading may incentivize task completion but can hinder accurate self-assessment and critical thinking, promoting a culture of compliance over genuine engagement
If students know the learning goals or targets that will be the basis for feedback and grading, they may focus solely on achieving those instead of seeking deeper challenges.	Some students aim mainly to meet learning objectives, which isn't necessarily negative. Providing clear learning targets empowers them to understand expectations without guessing.

Visible Learner Trait and Adult Mindframe Focus for Chapter 7

- **G**auge their current level of understanding.
- **R**eadiness to know where they are going and are confident to take on the challenge.
- **A**dapt tools to guide their learning.
- **D**etermine feedback and recognize that errors are opportunities to learn.
- **E**valuate their progress and adjust their learning.
- Be **S**uccessful in recognizing their learning and teach others.

VISIBLE LEARNERS GAUGE THEIR CURRENT LEVEL OF UNDERSTANDING

The "G" in the GRADES acronym for developing assessment capable visible learners stands for gauging their current level of understanding. Frey et al. (2018) noted that the first trait students need to develop to become a visible learner and drive their own learning is to *know* (gauge) their current level of understanding. Teachers must then embrace the notion that students bring a great deal to the classroom, and they are starting learning from scratch for every lesson (p. 23). Students that can *gauge* their current level of understanding are able to answer the three critical questions of a visible learner for every lesson or learning situation they are in:

1. What am I learning?
2. How will I know when I have learned it?
3. What's my next learning step? (Where to next)

This requires students to be aware of what the goals, targets, and ultimately the success criteria are for their learning for any lesson, task, assessment, or evaluation of their learning. When students are acutely aware of what they are supposed to learn, they are far more likely to focus on the processes that are supporting them to get to the established target and better determine their needs and the learning steps required.

Unpacking the Three Key Learning Questions

Effective feedback and grading hinge on three critical questions that drive the learning process. The first question, "Where am I going?" addresses a student's understanding of the learning goal for their current experience. Clarity around curriculum objectives is vital, enabling students to focus their efforts more effectively.

The second question, "How am I going?" involves assessing progress, whether through external evaluations by teachers, peers, or self-assessment. Providing clear success criteria is essential, as it allows students to measure their advancement toward the learning goal.

The third question, "Where to next?" is often the most challenging and essential for fostering student autonomy in learning. It emphasizes that learning is an ongoing process. However, traditional grading practices

(Continued)

(Continued)

frequently fail to support this crucial inquiry, often serving as a final judgment rather than a tool for growth. Effective grading should enhance, not hinder, a student's ability to drive their learning. As Hattie (2009, 2012) explains, this approach aligns with "Plus One" teaching, where feedback guides students to the next level of understanding and achievement, promoting a continuous cycle of improvement. •

Mindframes drive actions to support students in their ability to gauge their current level of understanding.

The beliefs of adults shape their actions, influencing student behaviors and achievement levels. Every student deserves at least a year's growth for a year's effort in teaching. It's essential for all educators to monitor student progress and growth actively. Two mindframes that align with developing students empower adults to make informed decisions about the tools and resources that support their learning paths:

- I am an evaluator of my impact on student learning.
- I am a change agent and believe all students can improve.

Teachers who view themselves as evaluators of their impact on student learning regularly assess and reflect on their effectiveness. Embracing a change agent mindset fosters a culture of continuous improvement, prompting the implementation of strategies that address individual needs and enhance student outcomes. This commitment allows students to better evaluate their understanding and identify strengths and areas for improvement through tailored feedback, unlocking their potential for growth.

Clarity Moves Grades Past Numbers Providing Explanation of Learning

Grades should accurately reflect learning rather than merely being numbers. Clarity is essential for understanding expectations, empowering teachers and students to address shortcomings, and giving purpose to education. Teachers must highlight the importance of learning to motivate students, emphasizing that grasping underlying concepts is more valuable than merely scoring high on tests. Grades should identify areas for improvement and guide both teachers and students on next steps. Effective communication throughout the learning process prevents confusion and enhances engagement with the curriculum. Ultimately, grades should foster continuous improvement and focus on comprehension, critical thinking, and the ability to apply knowledge in meaningful ways, shifting the focus from rote memorization to deeper understanding.

VIGNETTES

Sam is a ninth-grade student at Anywhere High School. For the most part, he is diligent about staying up with his classwork, homework, and so on. Like many students, he is much more engaged in topics he is passionate about. Ask him what subjects he likes the most, and English Language Arts and Social Studies will be the first ones mentioned. Ask him which subjects he's *not so excited about*, and he will say science and math. Sam does his best to keep himself caught up because he knows grades are important and his parents have instilled this in him.

Recently, he struggled to get through a unit on genetics, heredity, and probability in his biology class. Sam made sure to complete the homework assigned as much as he could, and prior to the unit test, he followed the study guide his teacher provided. He felt very prepared going into the test as he worked with a tutor his parents provided. On the day of the test, he felt confident that while he wasn't shooting for an A, he would be able to do pretty well and at least come in at a low B or B-. As he read through the questions and the prompts, he felt increasingly dejected and deflated. Sam did his best to answer as many questions and prompts as he could at first, but then he began to feel overwhelmed, which led to him feeling anxious, which ultimately led to frustration.

He walked out of class feeling dejected. He received a D- on his test with comments that said, "Sam, you really need to try harder!" He felt even more deflated and developed an apathy toward science that carried on with him the rest of his high school career causing him to stop taking any classes beyond what was required.

REFLECT AND CONSIDER

How similar is the previous scenario to anything you have experienced in your classroom(s)? How could the S (Support) in the SI²TE Model have been applied here to help Sam?

_____
_____
_____
_____
_____

CHAPTER 7 • GREAT LEARNERS GAUGE THEIR CURRENT LEVEL OF UNDERSTANDING

Multiple Levels of Clarity to Consider

As we aim to develop students who can assess their understanding, it's crucial for teachers and teams to clarify their goals for student achievement and align their instruction, assessment, feedback, and grading accordingly. **Standards:** Academic standards and outcomes should always be the starting point for teachers to determine their learning intentions and targets. Teachers can unwrap or deconstruct standards to provide a focused analysis of the skills, concepts, and rigor within each standard or outcome to establish an in-depth understanding of what students need to learn.

Skills (Practices): Different from the skills from standards or outcomes, these are methods and tactics students need to possess to perform tasks or assignments within certain domains. For example, mathematical or science and engineering practices would apply.

Dispositions: These are the traits and dispositions needed to develop visible learners, students who drive their learning. (See GRADES acronym and Chapter 12.)

VIGNETTES

Juxtaposition If Sam Was a Student at Wonder High School

Sam, a ninth grader at Wonder High School, usually approaches his classwork diligently. While he enjoys English Language Arts and Social Studies, math and science are less appealing to him. Nonetheless, he understands the importance of good grades, a value emphasized by his parents.

Recently, Sam struggled with a biology unit on genetics, heredity, and probability. He completed his homework, followed the study guide, and worked with a tutor, feeling prepared for the test and aiming for at least a B. Unfortunately, anxiety overwhelmed him during the test, leaving him feeling defeated.

The next day, Mrs. Johnson, his science teacher, noticed his distress and invited him to discuss his performance. Rather than simply pointing out mistakes, she highlighted his strengths and identified areas for improvement, reassuring him that struggling with new topics is common.

Mrs. Johnson provided specific feedback aligned with the unit's standards and success criteria. She praised his grasp of dominant and recessive traits but noted the need for more practice with Punnett squares and probability calculations. Additionally, she shared tailored strategies and connected him with a supportive study group. The Science PLC at Wonder High emphasizes collaborative learning, which is crucial for Sam's growth.

She allowed him to retake parts of the test, stressing that grades represent ongoing learning, not final judgments. Regular check-ins were scheduled to monitor his progress.

With this support, Sam regained his confidence and viewed his struggles as learning opportunities. By semester's end, he not only caught up with classmates but also developed a deeper appreciation for science, reflecting the benefits of a collaborative educational environment at Wonder High. ●

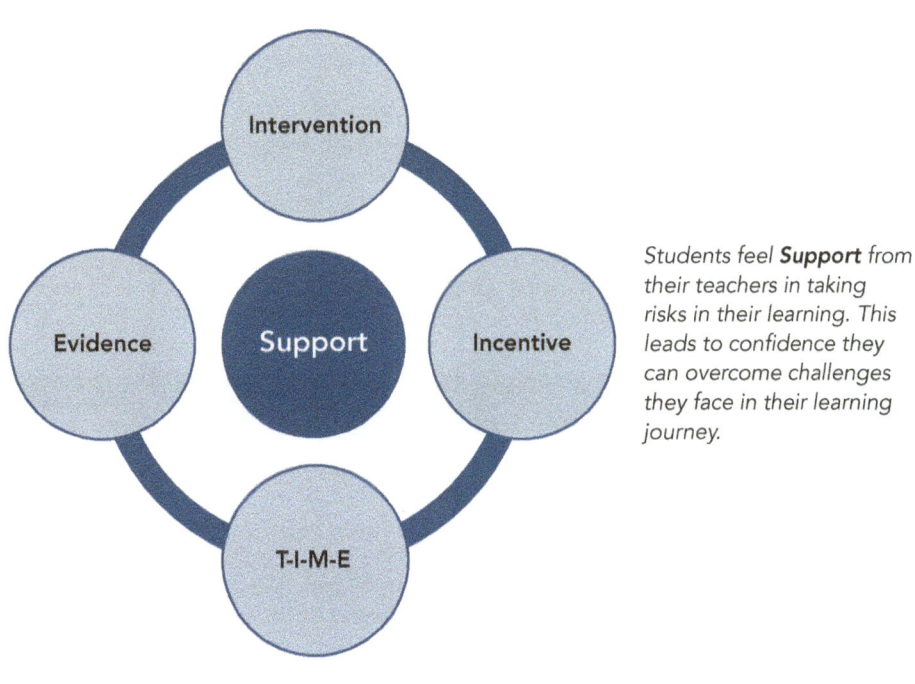

*Students feel **Support** from their teachers in taking risks in their learning. This leads to confidence they can overcome challenges they face in their learning journey.*

Applying the Clarity of Grading Scoring Guide to the Previous Scenario

The Clarity of Scoring Grading Matrix (CGSG; Figure 7.1) supports teachers to better align accuracy of feedback in the form of a grade related to the rigor of the task or performance. As the cognitive demands of tasks increase (SOLO Taxonomy through Surface, Deep, and Transfer of Learning) the value or weight in points, marks, or criteria given related to the grade will increase as well. As the change in color of the task boxes increases, this is a visual signal to help students gauge their current level of understanding and how it escalates and promotes a gradual yet stronger ability to know where they are in the learning process.

FIGURE 7.1: CLARITY OF GRADING SCORING GUIDE (CGSG)

Mindframes for Learning: Which Is a Focus for This Unit/Lesson I am an evaluator of my impact on student learning. I am a change agent and believe all students can improve.	*Visible Learner Trait* **Gauge** current level of understanding

	GENERATIVE LEARNING EXPERIENCES		WEIGHTED SCORING
SURFACE	**SOLO**-*The learner identifies isolated pieces of information and is unaware of any connections.* **Vocabulary and Concept Mapping (Unistructural)**	• Students define key terms (e.g., gene, allele, dominant, recessive, genotype, phenotype) and create a concept map linking the terms to show basic relationships in genetics.	0.5X
	SOLO-*The learner recognizes several information points related to a topic but lacks a clear understanding of how they are interconnected.* **Punnett Square Practice (Multistructural)**	• Students complete Punnett squares for single-trait crosses (monohybrid) using provided parental genotypes. They identify the possible genotypes and phenotypes of offspring without interpreting probability distributions.	X
	PRECIPICE OF COGNITIVE CHALLENGE		
DEEP	**SOLO**-*The learner comprehends the relationships and connections between related concepts and ideas.* **Case Study: Family Traits Investigation (Relational)**	• Students analyze family trait inheritance patterns using their own family (or a fictional pedigree chart). They explain how specific traits have been passed down and justify their reasoning using dominant/recessive principles.	1.5X
TRANSFER	**SOLO**-*The learner can extend and apply their knowledge to different contexts.* **Genetic Counseling Simulation (Extended Abstract)**	• Students take on the role of genetic counselors advising hypothetical parents about the probability of their child inheriting a specific genetic condition. They use Punnett squares, probability calculations, and real-world genetic data to explain risks and outcomes in a way that a non-scientist could understand.	2X

In the weighted scoring column on the right, the sample weighting guide helps teachers evaluate our impact on student learning and allows students to gauge their current understanding of the concepts and skills being taught, ultimately enhancing our communication through the grading process. How teachers ultimately score and keep track in their gradebooks will vary. Some teachers will use points or marks, some will use percentages, and still others will use some form of standards-based criteria. We will cite specific examples of teachers and teams applying each throughout the remaining chapters. X is used as the original base value and in this example, we will use (100) points. In a 100-point example X could be 20 points (10 + 20 + 30 + 40 = 100). We highlight X in that location because it informs the teacher and the student of their ability to gauge their learning because understanding and processing information is at the crux of true learning.

Clarity Minimizes Hodgepodge Grading

The challenge teachers face is how to incorporate these into lessons and instruction and to how to separate feedback and grading of them. Tom Guskey has spoken of the dangers of what he calls *hodgepodge grading*, when multiple and distinct factors are included into the determination of a single grade. Guskey notes that most computerized grading systems are based on traditional models that provide a single grade to be assigned to students. This forces teachers to condense diverse sources of evidence into a single number or symbol (Guskey, 2020).

VIGNETTES

Example of Hodgepodge Grading

Jill is a fifth-grade teacher at Anywhere Intermediate School. She is passionate about her students and provides them every opportunity to grow and develop as learners. She also loves her subject matter, which is science. During a recent unit focused on plants, Jill planned to address and support her students in mastering the following standards:

> 5-LS1-1: Support an argument that plants get the materials they need for growth chiefly from air and water.
>
> 5-LS2-1: Develop a model to describe the movement of matter among plants, animals, decomposers, and the environment.

As mentioned, Jill is very passionate about science and wants her students to love the subject matter as much as she does. Students engaged in deep learning about plants, their parts, reproduction, and how they grow, develop, and sustain life. She also attempted to support students in developing models in her science class to explain and develop arguments about science concepts.

(Continued)

(Continued)

One of her students, Jody, really enjoyed learning about plants and learned as much as she could about them but truly struggled on the assessment, which involved designing an experiment using a model to show how certain conditions allowed plants to thrive, simply survive, or die. Jody was able to demonstrate the content knowledge related to plants, their growth, and so on but truly struggled in using a model and developing a strong argument. When Jill averaged Jody's grade for the unit, she ended up with a C- for her overall grade (there were three components that were scored: concepts 85 percent, model and argument 50 percent, and participation 95 percent). The written feedback she received on the final assessment was that she needed to study more. She was also placed in an intervention group where the focus was on vocabulary understanding of concepts related to plants and movement of matter.

Jody lost some of her passion for science and especially plants. Even more so, she continued to struggle as the year went on related to using and explaining her understanding of science concepts related to using models. ●

The vignette about Jill's classroom is all too common, and it certainly doesn't reflect a lack of care from teachers regarding their students' learning. Teachers and teams must agree on the purpose of grading when determining students' grades. Grading actions must align and impact assessment and instructional decisions. Without doing so, grading can convolute where teachers and students need to go next in their learning

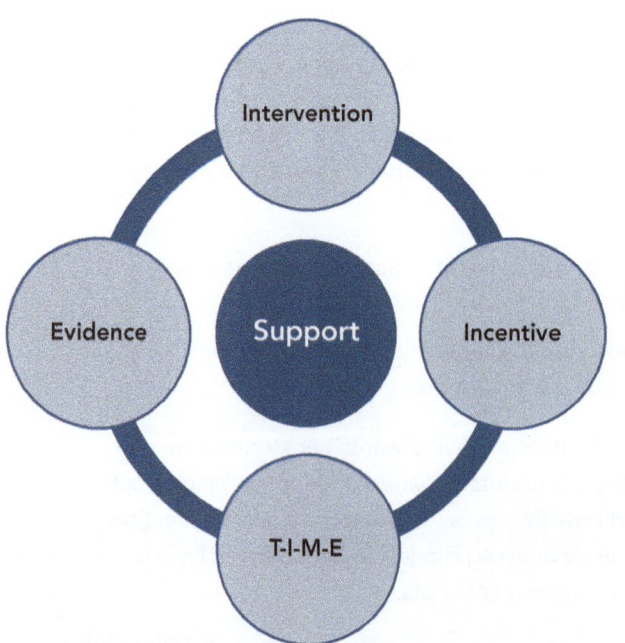

Evidence is a key in determining what success looks like and how both students and teachers know learning has taken place. Teachers must provide students with multiple avenues and opportunities to demonstrate evidence of their learning to prevent failure and build student resilience. Finally, teachers must not waste time gathering evidence unrelated to lessons and units' academic focus.

VIGNETTES

Addressing Jody's Struggles by Separating Behaviors From Academics

Jody, an enthusiastic student with a passion for plants, excelled in botanical concepts but struggled with an assessment requiring experimental design and modeling. Her grade of C- highlighted a mismatch between her content knowledge and her assessment performance. Initially, she was placed in a vocabulary-focused intervention, which failed to address her modeling and argumentation difficulties. Recognizing this, Jill implemented a targeted intervention, providing workshops on using models and explicit instruction on applying conceptual knowledge practically. Regular practice and tailored feedback helped Jody improve her modeling skills and arguments. Over time, her academic performance increased along with her grade, and her enthusiasm for science was rejuvenated!

Use Metacognition to Monitor Progress

Teachers can capitalize on the impact of metacognitive skills when students are taught to integrate them with contextual relevance of content, by experiencing learning strategies in authentic learning contexts, students develop a deeper appreciation for their utility and relevance, facilitating transferability across diverse academic domains. Several studies have shown the positive impact of metacognitive knowledge and metacognitive regulation on the students' achievement (Castro et al., 2014; Swanson, 1990).

Guskey has called for teachers to include three aspects of student performance into their grading structure: product, process, and progress (see Figure 7.2), and to consider a balance of all three when grading. In the opening vignette of this chapter, Joe Smith focused perhaps *too much* of his grading and feedback on the process(es) students were using to reach the goal of developing a quality argumentative essay and delivering or presenting to the class.

FIGURE 7.2: THREE CONSIDERATIONS WHEN GRADING

> **Product:** reflect how well students have achieved specific learning goals, standards, or competencies.
>
> **Process:** describe student behaviors that facilitate or broaden learning. These may be things that *enable* learning, such as formative assessments, homework, and class participation.
>
> **Progress:** show how much students have gained or improved. Sometimes these are referred to as "value-added" criteria. Although related to product criteria, progress criteria are distinct.

SOURCE: Adapted from Guskey (2018).

Progress is often not considered to the level it could or should be when grading decisions are made. Here is where teachers must cultivate students' metacognition, including their knowledge of strategies they are using related to the tasks they are engaging in. Again, clarity is essential as it allows students to perceive the difficulty of the task and steps required to be successful. This will help them make a better estimate and gauge where they are now and what their next learning steps are . . . even at the beginning. Promoting metacognitive awareness is essential to developing learners who can gauge their current level of understanding and accurately determine their strengths and plan to use strategies to move their learning forward.

VIGNETTES

Intentionally Teaching Students How to Learn

Mr. Carter, a fourth-grade teacher at Wonder Elementary School, introduces his class to metacognitive strategies, encouraging exploration without grade pressure. Students engage in a group discussion about the rock cycle and energy transfer, with Mr. Carter prompting questions to deepen their understanding. Afterward, they outline and summarize their findings on worksheets, organizing thoughts and recalling key concepts. Finally, students create graphic organizers, choosing formats like flowcharts or Venn diagrams to visualize the rock cycle. Reflecting on the activities, students express how discussions, outlines, and visualizations enhanced their comprehension. Mr. Carter concludes by affirming the value of these strategies across subjects. ●

Assessing in Advance of Instruction

One other strategy to support students to gauge their current understanding of upcoming learning intentions and to determine progress being made during a unit of study is assessing in advance of instruction. This allows both the students and the teacher to determine how and where to build on what students already know (Absolum, 2006, p. 25).

VIGNETTES

Returning to Joe Smith's seventh-grade social studies classroom, Joe, who recently joined Wonder Middle School, recognized the importance of clarity in assignments through collaboration with his PLC team and self-reflection. He aimed to assess and grade student progress throughout each unit. At the beginning of the next unit, he shared the five overarching learning targets for the upcoming weeks. He instructed his students to rate each target from 1 to 5, with 1 indicating an easy task and 5 indicating a challenging one. He also requested that they forecast their next learning steps. See Figure 7.3.

FIGURE 7.3: CLARITY AND DIFFICULTY ADVANCE ORGANIZER

WHICH WILL BE MOST CHALLENGING FOR YOU? RATING (1-5) 1 EASIEST, 5 HARDEST	CLARITY TARGETS	WHAT ACTIONS DO YOU NEED TO TAKE TO MEET THE TARGET?
	I understand that significant historical events in the United States have implications for current decisions and influence the future.	
	I can evaluate a public issue related to constitutional rights and the common good	
	I can research multiple perspectives to take a position on a current or historical issue for a paper of presentation.	
	I can evaluate the relevance of facts used informing a position on an issue or event.	
	I can engage others in discussions that attempt to clarify and address multiple viewpoints on public issues based on key details.	
	(Overarching for every unit) I can develop and defend an argument or claim and support it with quality evidence.	

Joe was pleased with his students' commitment to the task. He used a pre-assessment based on five clarity targets, along with a sixth target focused on argument development, present in every unit. Regular exit tickets facilitated self-assessment of daily progress. This approach allowed Joe to adjust instruction in real time, addressing his "expert blind spot" regarding students' misconceptions (Hattie & Zierer, 2017, p. 29). It enabled him to target instruction effectively and track progress on each learning target, which he included in his gradebook, sharing insights with his PLC for the benefit of his colleagues. See Appendix 7. ●

CHAPTER REFLECTION

1. In what ways have commonly held beliefs inhibited grading actions to be adjusted in your school or classroom?

2. When considering the four key components of teacher clarity, how can these help support effective scoring of student work to thus impact instructional planning?

3. How can we separate out behavioral dispositions from academic skills when scoring student work to impact student learning and support students' next steps?

NOTES

_____
_____
_____
_____
_____
_____
_____
_____
_____
_____
_____
_____
_____
_____
_____
_____
_____
_____

CHAPTER 8

Great Learners Are Ready to Take on Challenges

"The moment you doubt whether you can fly, you cease forever to be able to do it."

—J. M. Barrie

 **VIGNETTES**

A Meeting of the Minds

In a small conference room at Anywhere High School, the professional learning community (PLC) team convenes for their monthly meeting, feeling frustrated and as if their work is futile. Ms. Thompson, a veteran English teacher and team leader, expresses her concerns: "Our students aren't taking on challenges or setting goals. They don't seem to know how to demonstrate their learning, and I'm starting to think there's nothing we can do."

Mr. Patel, a math teacher with a decade of experience, echoes her sentiment. He explains that despite his efforts, such as breaking down problems and offering extra help sessions, the students don't see the value in pushing themselves.

Ms. Nguyen, an enthusiastic science teacher, notes that her students avoid setting challenging goals, settling for low, easily achievable ones. She feels as if she's hitting a wall.

Mr. Ramirez, known for his innovative teaching methods, adds, "Maybe they just don't have it in them. It's like we're speaking a different language."

(Continued)

(Continued)

Ms. Thompson, visibly discouraged, suggests that perhaps some kids just aren't cut out for this, acknowledging the same defeat reflected in her colleagues' faces.

As the meeting ends, the team is left with a mix of frustration and resignation. Their initial optimism has faded, leaving them questioning whether their belief in their students' potential was ever more than a hopeful illusion. ●

SUCCESS CRITERIA

As a reader, after reading this chapter I will be able to

1. Determine how to help students set challenging goals and achieving personal bests

2. Recognize that providing clear success criteria will support students to understand

    a. How to demonstrate their learning

    b. How they will be assessed in the form of a grade

3. Use success criteria as a driver for mastery learning/mastery grading

4. Use success criteria as a driver to promote desired learner behaviors ●

Visible Learner Trait and Adult Mindframe Focus for Chapter 8

- **G**auge their current level of understanding.
- **R**eadiness to know where they are going and are confident to take on the challenge.
- **A**dapt tools to guide their learning.
- **D**etermine feedback and recognize that errors are opportunities to learn.
- **E**valuate their progress and adjust their learning.
- **B**e Successful in recognizing their learning and teach others.

VISIBLE LEARNERS KNOW WHERE THEY ARE GOING NEXT AND ARE READY AND CONFIDENT TO TAKE ON THE CHALLENGE

We all aspire to prepare students to embrace challenges, pursue stretch goals, and be determined in their efforts. For this to happen, students must understand their learning objectives and identify their next steps, a crucial quality of visible learners. When students can articulate their next learning steps, they can respond effectively to three key questions: Where am I going? How am I going? And where to next? The third question encourages them to seek appropriate challenges. Teachers play a vital role in nurturing this capacity through classroom strategies, fostering both understanding and confidence in students.

In this chapter, we will explore three specific practices that teachers and collaborative PLC teams can implement:

- Helping students set challenging goals and personal bests
- Providing clear success criteria for how learning will be demonstrated and assessed
- Using success criteria to drive mastery learning and mastery grading

Mindframes drive actions to support students in their readiness to know where they are going and to be confident to take on the challenge.

Teachers with high expectations are more likely to connect new concepts with prior knowledge, use scaffolding techniques to support learning, provide more frequent and high-quality feedback, question frequently, and have a greater use of open-ended questioning (Hattie & Zierer, 2017, p. 132).

We believe the following two mindframes tightly align to developing students to make the best decisions as to the tools and resources they use to help them on their learning paths:

- I build relationships and trust so that learning can occur in a place where it is safe to make mistakes and learn from others.
- I give and help students understand feedback, and I interpret and act on feedback given to me.

Building relationships and trust between teachers and students creates a supportive learning environment where it is safe to make mistakes and learn from others. When teachers establish strong, positive connections with their students, they foster an atmosphere of mutual respect and openness. This foundation allows students to feel secure in taking risks and making errors, essential components of the learning process. Teachers who give clear, constructive feedback and help students understand and act on it guide students in recognizing their current standing and what steps to take next. This practice not only promotes a deeper understanding of the material but also boosts students' confidence and readiness to tackle future challenges, knowing they have the support and guidance they need to succeed.

COMMONLY HELD GRADING BELIEFS	COUNTERPOINT
Students know how they will be graded based on assignments they are given.	Grades are influenced by many factors, often undercommunicated through task instructions, leaving room for interpretation and ambiguity.
Students are simply motivated by points, and for that sometimes they need to be rewarded with them for simply completing work.	When this happens, it becomes a learned behavior. Primary students do not look at points and grades as a motivating factor. Instead, they often perform well based on their relationship with the teacher and the teacher's credibility. A frequently overlooked motivator is the promise of less work and more ownership for the next task.
We need to have a strict formula for grading to be fair.	Grading is subjective, and relying only on objective calculations *actually* fails to ensure fairness. A holistic approach that considers individual progress and understanding promotes equity and allows teachers to recognize students' unique strengths and improvements.

Setting Goals and Achieving Personal Bests Versus Performance Goals

Teachers should support students in setting challenging goals that inspire them to excel. When students set, monitor, and adjust their strategies, they develop resilience and readiness for future challenges. Learning goals provide specific improvement targets, with teachers supporting students through clear success criteria and a positive environment. These specific goals keep students focused on what they need to succeed, pushing them beyond their comfort zones. As Hattie (2023) states, setting situation-specific goals motivates students to exceed their past achievements and strive for mastery. Now, let's look at an example from a fourth-grade classroom.

VIGNETTES

Ms. Beth Coffman teaches fourth grade at Wonder Elementary, believing that perfect scores aren't always beneficial. She shares clear learning objectives and success criteria at the start of each lesson to guide grading and challenge students. This quarter, Beth focuses on goal setting, encouraging students to achieve personal bests while emphasizing concentration and perseverance. By prioritizing number sense and foundational math skills, she prepares students for more complex tasks and minimizes reliance on working memory. This is in line with Jenkins LtoJ® approach (https://www.crazysimpleeducation.com/about). Weekly timed multiplication tests emphasize accuracy over speed, building stamina while reducing cognitive load for challenging problems. She provided the following success criteria:

1. I can accurately multiply math facts.
2. I can concentrate and attend to precision when computing math problems.

This method helps students understand their learning progress and next steps, with grades reflecting their accuracy and effort.

> A = Above 90 or demonstrates *significant* improvement and progress that shows being on pace to achieve target (90) in very near future
>
> B = Above 80 or demonstrating improvement and progress that shows being on pace to achieve target (90)
>
> C = Above 70

STUDENT	INITIAL ASSESSMENT SCORE	WEEK 1 SCORE/ WEEK 2 GOAL	WEEK 2 SCORE/ WEEK 3 GOAL	WEEK 3 SCORE/ WEEK 4 GOAL	WEEK 4 SCORE/ WEEK 5 GOAL	*WEEK 5 SCORE*	STRAIGHT AVG.	OVERALL GRADE
Joe	87	No Score / 91	93 / 98	87 / 96	94 / 97	99	92%	A
Ashley	64	69 / 74	75 / 79	71 / 79	74 / 81	91	**74%**	A-
Brianna	37	51 / 60	55 / 61	61 / 64	71 / 80	75**	**59%**	C
Michael	65	61 / 68	78 / 83	No Score / 83	81 / 90	89	**75%**	A-
Duane	49	No score	37 / 51	55 / 60	75 / 80	96	**62%**	A

(Continued)

CHAPTER 8 • GREAT LEARNERS ARE READY TO TAKE ON CHALLENGES

(Continued)

STUDENT	INITIAL ASSESSMENT SCORE	WEEK 1 SCORE/ WEEK 2 GOAL	WEEK 2 SCORE/ WEEK 3 GOAL	WEEK 3 SCORE/ WEEK 4 GOAL	WEEK 4 SCORE/ WEEK 5 GOAL	WEEK 5 SCORE	STRAIGHT AVG.	OVERALL GRADE
Riley	61	51 / 70	No Score / 70	No Score / 70	68 / 74	No Score	Insufficient evidence	No Grade Currently
Dave	27	34 / 45	41 / 48	50 / 57	65 / 71	79**	49%	B
Steve	81	No Score	91 / 100	No Score	No Score	84	85%	B
Marc	61	71 / 89	74 / 80	No Score	68 / 71	87	60%	B+

(Straight average only includes actual scores)

Beth emphasizes the importance of mastering math facts and values student progress, focusing on how close students like Ashley, Michael, and Duane are to mastery *right now, and uses their current and most recent performance as a much stronger piece of evidence as opposed to any form of average. Instead of debating grades, Beth ensures Tier 2 or 3 interventions are based on specific evidence rather than using misleading averages of student performance. Her approach, supported by research, combines scores with qualitative evidence for informed decisions, prioritizing progress in grading and when needed providing practice and feedback instead of unneeded interventions.*

Important Footnote for Consideration

As discussed in Chapter 7, incorporating progress into grading is vital, as emphasized by Guskey (2022). Progress, a key element of visible learning research, should consistently influence grading and feedback. By combining quantitative and qualitative evidence, teachers can help themselves and students make informed decisions about the next steps in learning.

It could be debated whether or not some of these students should receive an A. We fully acknowledge that. Perhaps a B is more accurate to some. Our stance is simple, however, that none of these students, sans Riley who has simply not provided enough evidence to gauge her level of understanding and mastery, need Tier 2 or 3 interventions. Simply looking at their overall average scores could lead to erroneously thinking that. In addition, student progress for most demonstrates they are either at mastery or certainly on the cusp, and their grade is a much more accurate indicator. For example, let's consider Duane. Would we think his current attempt and score of 96, and grade of A is more or less accurate as to his average of 62%?

Reflect and Consider

What are some thoughts on using progress and goal setting as key factors in determining student grades?

_____

_____

_____

_____

_____

NOTE: See Appendix 8 for goal setting template examples.

Success Criteria as *the* Catalyst

For students to tackle challenges effectively, they need to know where they are in their learning and where they're headed. Success criteria provide the clarity to make this happen by showing students what mastery looks like (Hattie, 2023). While students may understand the lesson's purpose, (What am I learning?) they often don't know how their work will be judged or when they've succeeded, leading to a focus on completing tasks rather than true learning. Providing students with success criteria solves this issue by helping students answer the second and third key learning questions: How will I know I've learned it? What's next?

Success criteria (d = 0.64) link learning intentions to active student engagement. Teachers often present them as "I can" statements, which we will primarily use throughout the text, and are used to provide clarity for both the expected student outcomes and desired student behaviors. These criteria should guide instruction, assessment, *and grading*.

Besides "I can" statements, there are multiple other methods to provide students a roadmap of what success (criteria) would need to look like:

- We can
- SWBAT (Students will be able to)
- Rubrics or scoring guides
- Exemplars
- Modeled examples and guided practice

A key element is they need to represent actions, products, or performances students should demonstrate. Thus, they need to be concrete, measurable, and observable and, at times, up for negotiation. For example, "I can understand" or "I am learning to" are not in and of themselves measurable. Action words, such as list, describe, differentiate, explain, and so on can be measured. "Up for negotiation" simply means there will often be qualitative elements, such as strong textual evidence, optimal condition, compelling argument, and so on. See Figure 8.1.

FIGURE 8.1: EXAMPLES OF SUCCESS CRITERIA FOR STUDENT PRODUCTS AND PERFORMANCES

- I can cite the central idea of a text.
- I can identify key details to support the central idea.
- I can develop a compelling argument from evidence.
- I can determine strong evidence to support my claim.
- I can determine the slope of a line.
- I can defend or refute my hypothesis with distinct evidence from my experiment.
- I can generate a question using information from the text to ask myself, a peer, or teacher.
- I can subtract using two, 3-digit numbers with regrouping or without regrouping.
- I can add three, 2-digit numbers without regrouping or with regrouping.

When students have been made aware of success criteria they have the ability to determine their current level of learning as well their readiness level for next steps. Success criteria then become the drivers of classroom instruction, assessment, and feedback, as well as grading decisions for teachers.

CORE PRACTICE

At Wonder Middle School, the Science PLC team met to plan their upcoming unit on genetics and heredity, focusing on improving feedback and grading. They aimed to clarify success criteria for specific grades to guide instructional and assessment decisions.

Ms. Rivers emphasized defining clear success criteria for mastery that align with specific grades. Ms. Lee suggested challenging each other to establish criteria for different grades, ensuring grades reflect true student skills and knowledge. Mr. Garcia highlighted the need for aligned assignments to accurately assess understanding and guide next steps.

Ms. Rivers proposed mapping out success criteria before analyzing assignments (see Figure 8.2). The team agreed on thresholds for grading (e.g., B+ and above, below C+) to ensure reliability across classrooms. At the next meeting, they reviewed assignments, with Mr. Johnson discarding those that didn't align with the criteria. The team then adjusted assignments and tasks to ensure accurate grade calculations based on the established criteria. •

FIGURE 8.2: SUCCESS CRITERIA MAPPING

DESCRIPTION OF STUDENT PERFORMANCE	GRADE RANGE	DESCRIPTION OF WHAT STUDENTS CAN KNOW AND BE ABLE TO DO
High Level of Mastery	A to B+	All of what the B to C+ Criteria include as well as with limited to no support be able to do the following: <ul><li>Make solid predictions from analyzing and comparing data sets</li><li>Use models to generate and analyze data</li><li>Describe and predict how environmental factors affect the expression of traits and probability occurrences of traits in a population</li></ul>
Mastery	B to C+	Demonstrate mastery of some of the criteria listed in the A to B+ criteria or able to do with needed support as well as ability to do the following: <ul><li>Demonstrate solid understanding and application of key vocabulary and concepts<ul><li>Phenotype/Genotype</li><li>Meiosis</li><li>Genetic information</li><li>Mutations</li><li>Genetic variation</li></ul></li><li>Determine accurately genetic probability of traits being passed from parents to offspring as well</li></ul>
Below Mastery	C to D	Students can demonstrate mastery of some of the criteria listed in the A to B+ or B to C+ criteria or able to do so inconsistently or with adequate support
Well Below Mastery—Not Passing	F	Well below most, if not all, success criteria descriptions of concept and skill mastery listed above.

Template can be found in Appendix 9

Reflect and Consider

How do you or your PLC team determine what would be expected for specific grades (grade ranges) students receive?

_____
_____
_____
_____
_____

How could determining specifically what knowledge and skills students would have to master and demonstrate impact decisions such as assignments, tasks, and weighting of assessments? ●

_____
_____
_____
_____
_____

Aligning Success Criteria to Mastery Grading

FIGURE 8.3: ASSIGNMENT/TASK GRADING MATRIX

	Improvement of Learning and Achievement →	
Improvement of Grade ↑	**Coasting** Tasks lead to grade increases with no increase in learning or achievement	**Thriving** Increase of learning and achievement along with increase in academic grade
	Losing Grade either stays same or decreases with no increase in learning/achievement	**Developing** Learning/achievement increases without an increase in academic grade

Rewarding students with points, marks, or levels in a standards-based system for evidence of learning that doesn't align with their current mastery or success criteria is a significant disservice (i.e., "coasting"). We also challenge the idea that students are solely motivated by points and grades, suggesting they will only engage in work if it contributes to a predetermined amount of credit toward their final grade. We challenge this perpetuated belief because we have never seen nor heard of a first grader saying, "Hey, is this assignment worth at least 50? . . . Because if not, I'm not doing it!" That never happens, so *if* middle or high school students display this behavior of what some may call point gobbling, can we at least acknowledge it has been *learned?*

Mastery Learning

Mastery learning (d = 0.61) asserts that all students can eventually learn difficult material at their own pace if they clearly understand the learning intentions and success criteria. Key elements include a supportive learning environment, high collaboration, frequent and aligned teacher feedback, and correcting mistakes along the way. Mastery learning involves repeated lessons and continuous, personalized feedback loops to reinforce learning.

The concept traces back to John Carroll, who challenged the idea that aptitude divides students into "good" and "poor" learners. Carroll believed that given enough time and effective instruction, all students could achieve mastery, a view supported by Benjamin Bloom's research (Guskey, 2023).

 **VIGNETTES**

A Debate Among Spanish Teachers

In the faculty lounge at Everywhere High School, the Spanish department met amid tension over student comprehension.

Ms. Cortez, frustrated, lamented students' struggles with the subjunctive tense. Mr. Reed agreed, noting difficulties with basic conjugations and doubting some students' capabilities.

Department head Ms. Greenhall suggested rethinking their approach, emphasizing the need for more practice and reinforcement. Mr. Dorman proposed interactive activities like role-playing to help students internalize concepts.

Ms. Greenhall supported varied teaching methods and better assessments to guide learning. Mr. Reed agreed on focusing on quality assessments over time. Mr. Dorman shared success with mastery grading at Wonder High School.

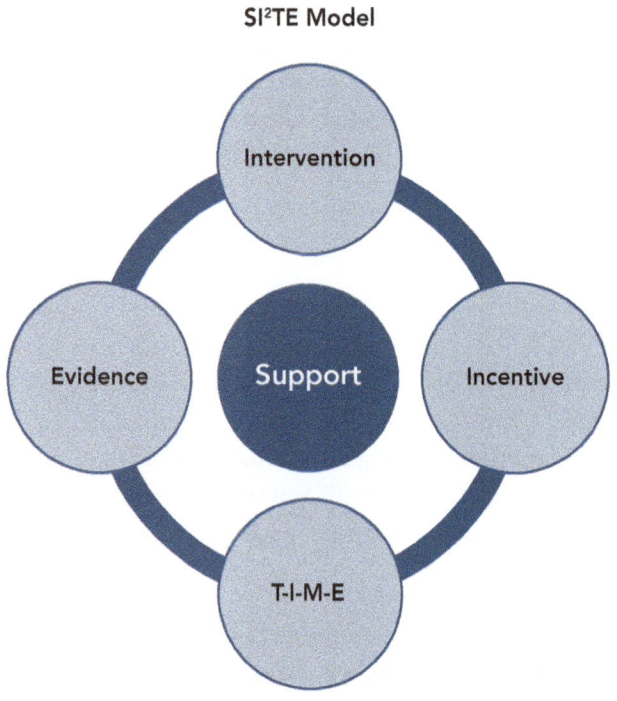

Time is a critical component in developing mastery learning. When we focus more on what the students are learning and the progress they are making toward curriculum targets as opposed to the time frame allotted, this helps teachers prevent unnecessary failure as well as develop solid academic skills in their students.

Bloom's model for mastery learning went a step further in calling for assessment evidence to be used formatively by the teacher and the student to correct errors and mistakes. Teachers then use assessment evidence to reteach certain portions of the curriculum students did not perform well on, and students have a chance to make adjustments in their learning. He proposed using mirrored assessments, where the concepts and ideas are the same, but the questions or prompts are different. Here, students are provided a second chance to not only demonstrate their learning to their teacher but also to themselves.

FIGURE 8.4: THE MASTERY LEARNING INSTRUCTIONAL PROCESS

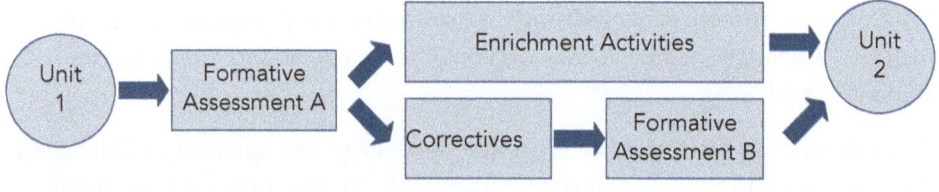

SOURCE: Reprinted from Guskey (2022).

For mastery learning to be effective, teaching must follow a structured sequence where students master each step before moving to the next. Students need a clear understanding of what they're expected to know and where they stand in their learning to bridge gaps. Clarity through well-defined success criteria is crucial.

Mastery learning works across ages and subjects, boosting motivation as students progress through clearly marked, incremental steps (see Figure 8.4).

Mastery Grading

We propose using mastery grading to align with mastery learning. Mastery grading combines standards-based learning with a pass-fail system (Guskey & Bailey, 2001). Teachers set clear thresholds for student work that demonstrates mastery of essential objectives. These thresholds provide concrete targets, helping students know when they've met success criteria and made progress. Work that falls short of these criteria receives no grade, instead students receive feedback for improvement before resubmitting. The focus remains on learning and progress, ensuring both teachers and students can track advancement toward goals. This concept of mastery grading has many benefits and supports students knowing where they are going in their learning journey. It also addresses the challenge teachers face when students perceive the goal is to gather as many points or marks as possible toward a final grade.

Readiness to Take on Next Challenge

Teachers face a dilemma when students try very hard to reach goals or targets and submit products that fall well below the mastery level. We can all remember having a student who put forth tremendous effort and simply handed in wretched work to which we gave them some indiscriminate points or marks such as 33 percent or 15 out of 40. Something that offers them *credit* for their effort that they "bank in the grade book" but does not in any way support them to know where they are going next in their learning (i.e., losing). They are simply being taught to throw points into the pot and hope that it adds up to something of quality later.

Figures 8.5a and 8.5b highlight our model of mastery grading. Teachers determine a minimum threshold of proficiency that is shared with students. Students must demonstrate evidence that would indicate they are on pace for *potential mastery,* meaning they are demonstrating in their work a level aligned to concepts and skills embedded in the criteria provided. Figure 8.5a demonstrates a teacher using numerical point values to calculate and determine the grade, while Figure 8.5b demonstrates a teacher using a more standards-based type of reporting in their grade book with the criteria being T for thorough understanding and P for partial. The yellow line represents a metaphoric or conceptual line of the threshold students have to demonstrate significant progress in their learning before any aspect of a grade is provided to them. If they do not meet that level of progress, students receive feedback and something in the gradebook is placed such as IP (in progress) to convey to students and parents they have submitted work or performance, but it is not yet on track toward mastery to receive any form of a grade yet.

FIGURE 8.5A: MASTERY GRADING USING NUMERICAL POINT VALUES

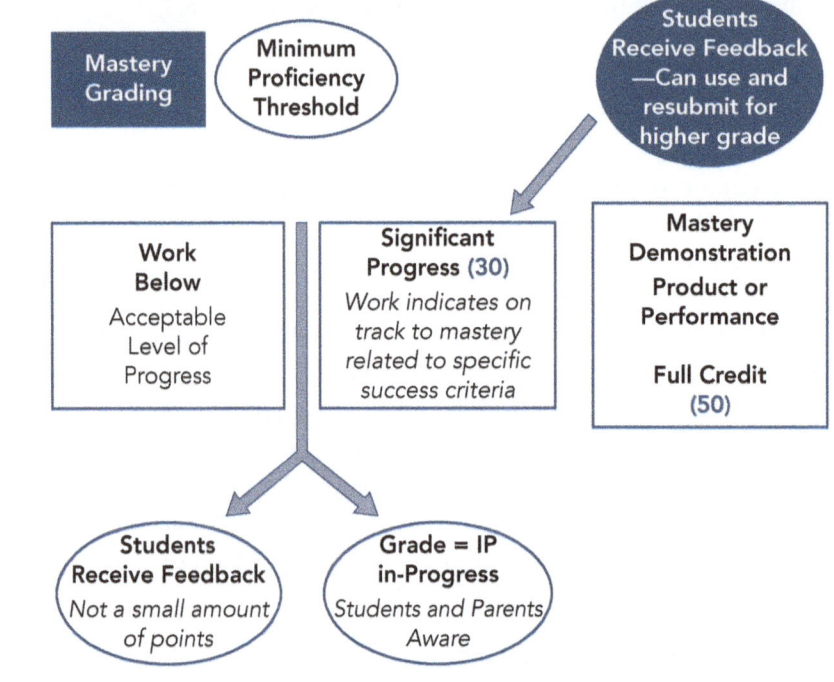

FIGURE 8.5B: MASTERY GRADING USING STANDARDS-BASED REPORTING

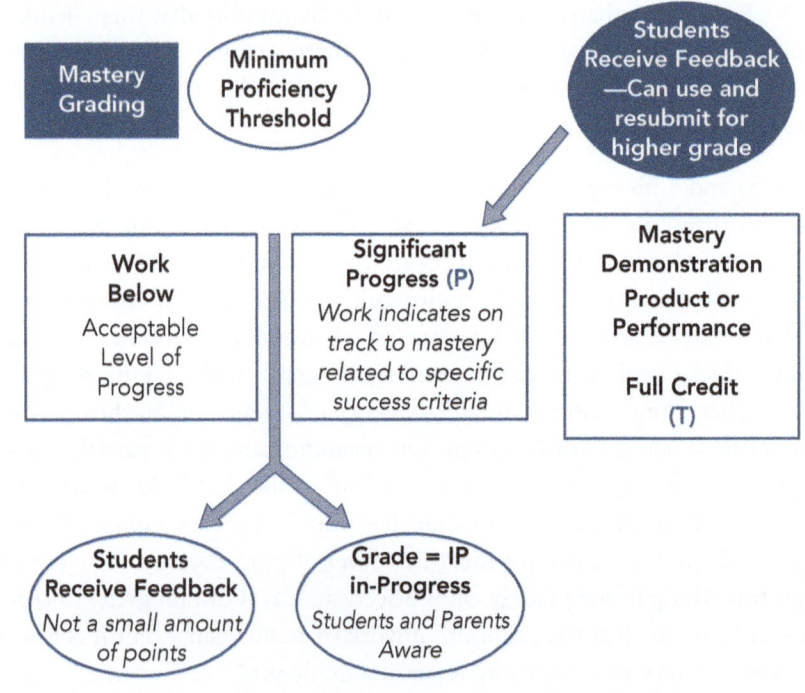

CORE PRACTICE

Joan Marquette and Aaron Medveseck, seventh-grade English Language Arts (ELA) teachers at Wonder Middle School, collaborate with their PLC team on teaching, assessment and grading. The team prioritizes standards based on endurance, leverage, and readiness (Ainsworth, 2011). They selected eight standards for year-long focus and developed universal learning success criteria applicable across any unit. This approach, combined with mastery grading, helps students track their progress and prepare for new challenges.

> **Standard: RI 7.2:** Determine two or more central ideas in a text and analyze their development over the course of the text; provide an objective summary of the text.
>
> **Learning Intention:** Use tools, resources, and strategies to understand and explain what the text is conveying to the reader.

Success Criteria

- Identify two central ideas of text
- Identify 3-4 key details that support the central idea
- Describe how each key detail supports the central idea
- Develop an objective and terse summary

Both teachers share success criteria with their students and also share with them how they will be graded before each unit. Joan uses a point system when compiling grades for her students, while Aaron uses more of a standards referenced approach in his grade book.

SUCCESS CRITERIA	CONSIDERATIONS FOR MINIMUM/MASTERY GRADING
1. Identify two central ideas of text 2. Identify 3–4 key details that support the central idea 3. Describe how each key detail supports the central idea 4. Develop an objective and terse summary	Students must identify at least one central idea from the text, at least one detail that supports the central idea, and justification as to what detail supports the central idea. • In Joan's class, this allows students to acquire thirty of the fifty points possible. • In Aaron's class, this allows students to receive a P which stands for progressing toward or partial mastery, while a T stands for full mastery.

(Continued)

(Continued)

Both teachers had students that struggled to meet the minimum criteria, met the minimum threshold, or were able to master all of the criteria. The following are how the teachers monitored this in their grade books as well as some next steps in supporting their students in where to go next.

Joan's Class–Traditional Grading System of points and marks with an emphasis on mastery grading and considering students' current and most recent level of performance as well as a full eradication of any averaging of grades. She uses IP for work that is not showing adequate progress toward mastery or proficiency yet.

STUDENTS	CRITERIA MET	CURRENT GRADE IN GRADEBOOK	NEXT STEPS
Marcia	1-2	35/50	Practice working on connecting key details back to central idea and developing summary
Josh	ALL four	50/50	Choice in next task* (Incentive from SI²TE)
Jacqueline	1 (Identified two central ideas but no key details)	IP (In progress)	Practice and feedback working on connecting key details
Dave	None (work submitted)	IP (In progress)	Small group intervention in class to work on identifying central ideas from text
Teasha	1-2-4	35/50	Practice working on connecting key details back to central idea
Jose	All four	50/50	Choice in next task* (Incentive from SI2TE)
Blase	None submitted	0*	Phone call/email home
Mark	1-2-3	35/50	Practice on summarization and feedback

Aaron's Class-Standards Referenced Approach

T = Thorough understanding and application of grade-level concepts and skills

Q = Adequate understanding and application of grade-level concepts and skills

P = Partial (or progressing) understanding and application of grade-level concepts and skills

IP = In progress—Used during units of study where work or performance is at or just above minimal

M = Minimal understanding and application of grade-level concepts and skills

N = No evidence of understanding and application of grade-level concepts and skills

NWS = No work product or performance submitted

STUDENTS	CRITERIA MET	CURRENT GRADE IN GRADEBOOK	NEXT STEPS
Karen	1-2	Q	Practice working on connecting key details back to central idea and developing summary
Liz	ALL four	T	Choice in next task* (Incentive from SI²TE)
Mackenzie	1 (Identified two central ideas but no key details)	IP (In progress)* (Would be an M)	Practice and feedback working on connecting key details
Tony	None (work submitted)	IP (In progress)* (Would be an N)	Small group intervention in class to work on identifying central ideas from text
A'ieasha	1-2-4	Q	Practice working on connecting key details back to central idea
Aida	All four	T	Choice in next task* (Incentive from SI²TE)
Tommy	No work submitted	NMS 0**	Phone call/email home
Jacob	1-2-3	Q	Practice on summarization and feedback

*Grades for Mackenzie and Tony currently are IP in the gradebook that is accessible to parents and students as their work submission is not yet showing progress towards potential mastery. (The N and M represent their current level that Aaron is aware of.)

**The zero is because there is no current evidence of mastery but will not necessarily be averaged later into final grade determination. ●

Aligning mastery learning and grading with specific success criteria drives both grades and assessment evidence, helping teachers determine the support students need. In addition, students become more acutely aware of the expectation for mastery and how they will be graded.

Reflect and Consider

For an upcoming unit of study, what are the success criteria? Which of them are essential for students to demonstrate some degree of mastery to know they are progressing toward the unit's overall goals? How could that become the basis for mastery grading? ●

_____
_____
_____
_____

Using Grading to Inform Next Learning Steps

Grades should inform both the students and the teacher what their (students) next learning steps are. Brookhart (1991) identified hodgepodge grading, where the students' grade was a combination of achievement, effort, growth, attitude or class conduct, homework, and class participation. We equate that to *coasting* in the Assignment/Task Grading Matrix (see Figure 8.3). When all of these factors are not just considered but factored into the final grade without any specific guidance on how to separate them, it provides no real evidence to determine *where we go next*.

CORE PRACTICE

The civics team at Wonder High School planned lessons on the presidential primary elections and prioritized standards on political roles and writing arguments. They developed universal success criteria for analyzing evidence and making claims, ensuring these skills are emphasized across units. This approach helps students track their progress and understand how to advance, regardless of the specific context.

Priority Standard: Analyze the roles and activities of political parties, interest groups, and mass media and how they affect the beliefs and behaviors of local, state, and national constituencies.

9-10.WS.1 *Write arguments focused on* discipline-specific content.

Introduce precise claim(s), distinguish the claim(s) from alternate or opposing claims, and create an organization that establishes clear relationships among the claim(s), *counterclaims*, reasons, and evidence.

Success Criteria for Unit

**(Universal criteria used for every unit).

- *Analyze evidence from multiple sources to make strong claims (arguments)****
- *List and expand upon 1-2 possible counterpoints to your claims (arguments)****
- *Determine the power and limitations of political parties, interest groups, and mass media*
- *Identify possible (likely) beliefs of two or more constituent groups*
- *Indicate specific examples of how constituent beliefs drive their actions and behaviors*

Students were assigned the following task with aligned criteria after a few days of instructional activities. Students were also provided point values for each of the criteria.

Short Constructed Response Item

Considering the results of the 2024 presidential primary election, develop a short 2-3 paragraph piece explaining how constituent beliefs may have been affected by political parties, interest groups, and mass media.

- Identify overarching beliefs of political parties and interest groups closely involved w/the primary elections of 2024 **(30)**
- Identify 2-3 common constituent beliefs related to their party affiliation (10)
- State, w/examples, 2-3 constituent behaviors likely influenced by mass media activities (10)
- Explain, w/examples, how interest groups reached voters and impacted the candidates they supported with evidence (10)

(Continued)

The civics team focuses on key learning aspects for each lesson to effectively monitor their 467 students' progress using clear criteria. They sought to identify which students could accurately recognize the beliefs of political parties and interest groups, as this is essential learning needed for future units. By employing weighted scoring, they classified student work into two groups: scores of 40 and above indicated a solid understanding, while those below 40 required intervention. This method quickly informed their instructional actions and helped guide students on their next learning steps. ●

Reflect and Consider

How do you determine as a teacher what the grades tell you about specific skills students are or are not demonstrating? How do your grading actions help the students know their current level of understanding? ●

_____

_____

_____

_____

_____

Success Criteria: For Desired Behaviors

Developing visible learners who drive their learning involves supporting students in seeing themselves as their own teacher and focusing on *actions* that drive their learning. That is why we have chosen the GRADES acronym aligned to the six traits of assessment capable visible learners (Hattie & Zierer, 2017).

Dave was recently in a school conducting student interviews and asking middle school students questions about learning. One was, "what makes a good learner a good learner?' Most of the comments were compliance-based: stay quiet in class, pay attention, follow directions, and don't mess around. Those are the traits of a good kid (and both of us wish we had them in our houses more often), but they are not really what makes a good learner. That morning, during the announcements, the principal shared that, "all learners in our school need to be resilient, curious, collaborators, risk takers, and ones who see error as a path to learning and seek feedback to grow and develop." It was obvious this was something that is shared daily during morning announcements. Dave asked the students why they didn't mention any of the traits referred to during announcements. Their responses included, "we don't even think about those. It's like the pledge of allegiance, we say the words by heart, but don't really think about them!" (See Appendix 10 for examples of learner dispositions.)

A strong consideration and recommendation is to have (at least) two criteria for every lesson: One for the product or academic performance *and* one for the behaviors we hope students to demonstrate from that lesson (see Figure 8.6).

FIGURE 8.6: EXAMPLE QUALITY SUCCESS CRITERIA

- I can collaborate with my peers to solve a complex problem.
- I can participate actively in discussions.
- I can share my thinking with a peer or teacher.
- I can persevere when solving difficult problems.
- I can attend to precision when solving math problems.
- I can use resources when trying to learn something on my own.
- I can show persistence and concentration when close reading documents.

Science and math teachers can also lean on the standards of mathematical practice as well as the science and engineering practices put out by the National Science Teaching Association (Figure 8.7)

FIGURE 8.7: NATIONAL SCIENCE TEACHING ASSOCIATION MATHEMATICAL PRACTICES AND SCIENCE AND ENGINEERING PRACTICES

STANDARDS OF MATHEMATICAL PRACTICES	SCIENCE AND ENGINEERING PRACTICES
1. Make sense of problems and persevere in solving them.	1. Asking questions (for science) and defining problems (for engineering)
2. Reason abstractly and quantitatively.	2. Developing and using models
3. Construct viable arguments and critique the reasoning of others.	3. Planning and carrying out investigations
4. Model with mathematics.	4. Analyzing and interpreting data
5. Use appropriate tools strategically.	5. Using mathematical and computational thinking
6. Attend to precision.	6. Constructing explanation (for science) and designing solutions (for engineering)
7. Look for and make use of structure.	7. Engaging in argument from evidence
8. Look for and express regularity in repeated reasoning	8. Obtaining, evaluating and communicating information

CHAPTER REFLECTION

1. How could you incorporate student goal setting and achieving personal bests into grading actions?

2. What is the current reality of how success criteria is developed and shared with students? How could this support students in determining how they will be assessed in the form of grades and determining their next learning steps?

3. How could success criteria be used to implement master learning/mastery grading in your school or classroom?

4. How could you use success criteria as a driver to promote learner behaviors?

NOTES

CHAPTER 9

Great Learners Adapt Tools to Guide Their Learning

"It is essential to have good tools, but it is also essential that the tools should be used in the right way."

—Wallace D. Wattles

 **VIGNETTES**

Joan Smith, a ten-year veteran ninth-grade English Language Arts (ELA) teacher at Wonder High School, is committed to her students' success. She understands many freshmen lack the readiness skills needed for high school success. Her current unit focuses on effective writing processes.

Joan's grading style emphasizes the importance of completing each task with quality to reach the final learning target. In a recent unit, her students read *To Kill a Mockingbird* and wrote an argumentative essay on which character—Scout, Atticus, or Jem—developed the most. This project involved three tasks:

1. Graphic Organizer (50%)—Students had to complete this before starting their essay.
2. Rough Draft (20%)—A preliminary version of their essay.
3. Final Essay (30%)—Demonstrated improvements based on feedback.

(Continued)

(Continued)

Joan believes in giving students ownership of their learning, allowing them to choose their focus character. This structured approach ensures students understand the importance of each step in the writing process and helps them develop critical writing skills.

Argumentative Essay Graphic Organizer

1. Introduction
   - Hook
   - Background information on character
   - Thesis statement
   - For body paragraphs 1-2-3
2. Topic Sentence
   - Evidence/support 1
   - Explanation
   - Counterargument
   - Rebuttal, if applicable
3. Conclusion
   - Restate thesis
   - Summary of main points
   - Closing statement:

Joan always seeks student feedback after unit tests and projects to improve her teaching and assess her impact. The graphic organizer used in a recent essay assignment elicited mixed responses:

- "The graphic organizer was a nice starter tool but felt like a hoop to jump through."
- "The criteria helped me complete the task more than the graphic organizer."
- "Without the graphic organizer, I would have been lost, but the criteria guided my learning."
- "The graphic organizer slowed me down. I prefer my own method and only did it for the points."

- "I made my own tool instead of using the graphic organizer, which helped me more."

- "I completed the graphic organizer because it was worth 50 points."

Sampling Scores of Several Students

STUDENT	GRAPHIC ORGANIZER	ROUGH DRAFT	FINAL ESSAY	TOTAL SCORE/ GRADE
Kristen	50	20	15	85 B
Brittany	20	15	30	75 C
Mark	20	20	30	70 C-
Gabe	50	0	30	80 B-
Samantha	50	20	25	90 A

As Joan compared final essay scores to overall grades, she noticed mixed results. For some students, high graphic organizer scores correlated with strong final essays and grades. However, for many, there was no correlation or even a decrease. The survey results provided mixed feedback: Some students found the three tasks helped them coalesce their ideas, while others felt the graphic organizer was too constricting. Some believed they could have used the criteria to start their rough drafts directly, and others felt that working through the graphic organizer brought them closer to a final draft. ●

SUCCESS CRITERIA

As a reader, after reading this chapter I will be able to

1. Determine grading and feedback actions that promote students being able to adapt and guide their learning

2. Apply the visible learning mind frames of collaborating with peers and students about my conceptions of progress and engaging as much in dialogue as monologue

3. Determine ways to empower students through metacognition, reflection, and strategy monitoring to adapt tools to guide their learning

4. Avoid early grading by using training tasks to support students in developing key skills needed to develop deeper levels of mastery ●

Alignment to Success Criteria Is Critical

When designing meaningful tasks, teachers must ensure they align with success criteria, providing evidence of students' mastery or progress. The Clarity of Grading Scoring Guide (CGSG) (see Figure 9.1) maintains focus on evidence and feedback from tasks, guiding appropriate grading weights based on cognitive demand. Joan emphasizes using graphic organizers and essay drafts not merely as hoops for students to jump through but as tools to organize their thoughts. She encourages viewing errors as learning opportunities and values peer collaboration. Joan uses graphic organizers as a feedback platform for most students, allowing them to receive input before writing their essays. Others may prefer feedback once engaged with their drafts. By using student feedback, she adjusts assignment scoring to focus on progress toward successful argumentative essays. The CGSG helps her tailor point distribution to align with task requirements while allowing students to earn points through revisions in small groups. This approach promotes effective time management and growth in writing skills, establishing supportive scoring and grading actions (see Figure 9.1).

It's Not an Either/Or but an And/Or

Students' final scores should reflect their performance on the final essay while fostering and not overlooking their ability to organize ideas throughout the process. Growth in communication skills, which is what writing an argumentative essay is all about, is essential and shouldn't be overlooked, even if these were developed in the planning phase (developing their graphic organizer). Genuine feedback aligned with their learning should take precedence over simply adding points to a gradebook. If some students learn more while completing their graphic organizers and others develop more while writing their final essays, they should not be penalized with a lower score or inaccurate feedback. If the goal is to write a strong argumentative essay based on criteria, and students can do this, they shouldn't be penalized for not adhering strictly to a predetermined process, just as those demonstrating organizational skills early should receive credit for their progress. See scoring in Figure 9.1

FIGURE 9.1: CLARITY OF GRADING SCORING GUIDE (CGSG)

Mindframes for Learning: Which Is a Focus for This Unit/Lesson I collaborate with my peers and my students about my conceptions. I engage as much in dialogue as monologue.	*Visible Learner Trait* **Adapt** tools to guide their learning	
GENERATIVE LEARNING EXPERIENCES		**WEIGHTED SCORING**
SURFACE	**Graphic Organizer (teacher or student version)**	0.5X
	Clarity and organization: The graphic organizer is highly clear and meticulously organized, demonstrating a logical and cohesive flow of ideas.	25pts
	Completeness: The graphic organizer is comprehensive and thorough, including detailed main ideas and well-supported supporting details.	
	Logical flow: The graphic organizer exhibits a highly logical flow of ideas, with seamless transitions between main ideas and supporting details that enhance coherence and understanding.	
PRECIPICE OF COGNITIVE CHALLENGE		
DEEP / **TRANSFER**	**Rough Draft of Essay/Final Draft of Essay**	1.5X
	Introduction	75pts up to the full credit 100 pts
	Hook: The hook is exceptionally compelling, effectively drawing the reader into the essay and clearly relating to the topic in a unique and engaging way.	
	Background information on character: Thorough and insightful background information is provided, demonstrating a deep understanding of the character's context and its significance to the thesis statement and argument.	
	Thesis statement: The thesis statement is exceptionally clear, precise, and compelling, effectively outlining the argumentative stance of the essay with specific previews of the main points that will be elaborated on.	
	Body Paragraphs	
	Topic Sentence: Exceptionally clear and focused topic sentences succinctly introduce and outline the main point of each paragraph, demonstrating a strong organizational structure.	
	Evidence/support 1: Compelling and well-chosen evidence or support is provided that effectively reinforces and substantiates the topic sentence and thesis statement, demonstrating a deep understanding of the argument.	
	Explanation: Exceptionally detailed and insightful explanation of evidence thoroughly connects back to the argument being made, showcasing a sophisticated understanding of the topic and argumentative strategies.	
	Counterargument: Counter arguments are skillfully acknowledged and effectively addressed, showcasing a nuanced understanding of multiple perspectives and enhancing the credibility of the argument.	
	Conclusion	
	Restate thesis: The thesis statement is restated clearly and compellingly, providing a succinct summary that reinforces the essay's argumentative stance.	
	Summary of Main Points: Exceptionally clear and insightful summary of main points provides a compelling overview that strengthens the overall argument and leaves a lasting impact.	
	Closing Statement: The closing statement is exceptionally strong, providing a memorable conclusion that reinforces the essay's argumentative stance and leaves a powerful impact on the reader.	

Reflect and Consider

What are some reflections related to the vignette on Joan's ELA class?

_____
_____
_____
_____
_____

COMMONLY HELD GRADING BELIEFS	COUNTERPOINT
Simply completing work, including following certain processes for doing so, should be an important aspect of grading.	Grading should focus on understanding and innovation, not just task completion. Overemphasizing process adherence can stifle creativity and discourage unique problem-solving.
Students should be graded on each task as a separate entity	Grading each task separately can obscure progress and growth, leading to a focus on task completion rather than integrated and deeper learning.
I have to grade everything, or kids won't do it	Grades are feedback, but points and marks rarely motivate students. Providing opportunities for ownership and progress toward mastery often serves as a more effective motivator.
It's not fair if I give students the same grade when one needed three opportunities to reach mastery and another only needed one	Grading should focus on equal opportunity, not equal chances. Multiple opportunities for assessment boost comprehension and mastery, supporting diverse learning paces and valuing persistence and improvement.

Visible Learner Trait and Adult Mindframe Focus for Chapter 9

- **G**auge their current level of understanding.
- **R**eadiness to know where they are going and are confident to take on the challenge.
- **A**dapt tools to guide their learning.

- **D**etermine feedback and recognize that errors are opportunities to learn.
- **E**valuate their progress and adjust their learning.
- Be **S**uccessful in recognizing their learning and teach others.

VISIBLE LEARNERS ADAPT TOOLS TO GUIDE THEIR LEARNING

The "A" in the GRADES acronym emphasizes how students who drive their learning can adapt tools to guide them in doing so. Visible learners actively engage in enhancing skills to advance their learning. A student who is capable of adapting tools to guide their learning is learning how to learn and over time able to practice learning. Students who drive their own learning select from various strategies, techniques, or resources. Students' decision-making skills are bolstered by creating opportunities for them to reflect on how *they learn best*.

Teaching students effective practice, study, and learning strategies is essential for academic success. Students should learn to choose the right tools for each task, fostering versatility and resilience. Avoiding early grading supports reflective practice, helping students understand critical learning progressions and achieve larger goals. Reflective practices enhance understanding and metacognitive skills, enabling students to monitor and regulate their learning processes effectively.

We will focus in the chapter on specific grading actions teachers can take to support students in adapting tools to guide their learning, such as the following:

- Strategy monitoring self-judgment and reflection
- Avoiding early grading
- Use of training tasks ●

Mindframes drive actions to support students in adapting tools to guide their learning.

All educators must have the ingrained belief that it is us that causes learning. We must be vigilant to monitor both the actions we are taking that are moving our students toward desired behaviors and learning outcomes, as well as those that move them away from them. Frey et al. (2018) notes that how teachers think about their impact and student progress is essentially most relevant to their students' success (p. 26). The following are two mindframes that we believe align to developing students so that they can make the best decisions as to the tools and resources they use to help them on their learning paths:

- I collaborate with my peers and my students about my conceptions of progress and my impact.
- I engage as much in dialogue as monologue.

Teachers must take time to listen to their students and engage in the type of dialogue that promotes a partnership between teacher and student. Some of this *dialogue* occurs by examining student work and performance to help students determine their next learning steps as well as the next adult actions needed in the classroom. Teachers must elicit and gather student voice evidence related to how students feel about their learning journeys and how they are actively supporting them. Next and even more importantly we need to *act* upon that evidence and make the right kinds of adjustments in our strategies and practices.

In Joan's example, she took time to listen to her students and the comments they provided her related to the task. She also used feedback from her students about their progress and her impact and made necessary adjustments in her practices. She embodied these two mindframes mentioned.

Supporting Students in Adapting Tools to Guide Their Learning

Teachers and collaborative teams can develop specific instructional and grading actions to increase students' ability to adapt tools to guide their learning. In doing so, there are several high-level influences to consider and practices that align to them.

Strategy Monitoring

In demanding classrooms, integrating effective learning strategies into daily teaching, assessing, and grading is crucial for student success. Strategy monitoring ($d = 0.53$) involves students overseeing their methods to achieve goals. Teaching problem-solving and monitoring skills helps students apply strategies effectively. By embedding these strategies into the curriculum, educators promote consistency and ensure all students have equitable access to essential learning tools, fostering self-regulated learners.

Self-Judgment and Reflection

Self-assessment or judgment (d = 0.81) of one's current level of mastery plays a crucial role in independent learning. Students often struggle to accurately gauge their own abilities. Teachers need to help students develop the skill of objectively evaluating their work according to established standards. This skill is known by various terms in academic circles, such as *evaluative knowledge* or *informed judgment*, but the emphasis remains on the students' ability to reflect on their work, compare it to standards, and make informed self-assessments (Visiblelearningmetax.com).

VIGNETTES

In Mr. Thompson's eighth-grade ELA class at Wonder Middle School, students wrote persuasive essays. To improve their outlines, Mr. Thompson used a strength-based rubric that focused on rewarding key elements of a well-constructed outline. This approach encouraged students to monitor their strengths and guided their growth, rather than penalizing errors.

The scoring matrix included criteria, such as the following:

- **Clear thesis statement:** Is the main argument clearly stated and supported by the outline?
- **Logical organization:** Does the outline follow a clear and coherent structure, with main points and supporting details logically arranged?
- **Effective use of evidence:** Does the outline include specific examples, facts, or quotations to support the main points?
- **Comprehensive coverage:** Does the outline address all key aspects of the topic, considering multiple perspectives and potential counterarguments?
- **Clarity and conciseness:** Is the outline written in clear, concise language, with each point expressed succinctly and precisely?

For each criterion, Mr. Thompson provided a description of what exemplary, proficient, developing, and beginning performance would look like. He also included specific examples and guiding questions to help students understand how they could meet or exceed expectations for each criterion. See Figure 9.2.

During the outlining process, Mr. Thompson advised students to use the rubric to assess their performance and plan their next steps. He emphasized that the goal was to refine their outlining skills, not just to earn points. Before starting, he asked students to reflect on their experience with outlining essays, considering recent work they've done.

(Continued)

(Continued)

FIGURE 9.2: MR. THOMPSON'S ASSESSMENT RUBRIC

CRITERIA	BEGINNING 1	DEVELOPING 2	PROFICIENT 3	EXEMPLARY 4
Clear Thesis Statement	Thesis is unclear or missing.	Thesis is present but vague or unfocused.	Thesis is clear but may lack some detail.	Thesis is clear, detailed, and focused.
Logical Organization	Outline lacks structure; points are disorganized.	Outline has some structure but is unclear in places.	Outline is mostly clear and well-organized.	Outline is clear, coherent, and logical.
Effective Use of Evidence	Little to no evidence is provided.	Some evidence is provided but lacks relevance or specificity.	Good use of relevant evidence.	Excellent use of specific, relevant evidence.
Comprehensive Coverage	Key aspects are missing; single perspective.	Some key aspects are addressed; limited perspectives.	Most key aspects are covered; multiple perspectives considered.	All key aspects are thoroughly covered; multiple perspectives and counterarguments are considered.
Clarity and Conciseness	Language is unclear and verbose.	Language is somewhat clear but wordy.	Language is clear and mostly concise.	Language is clear, concise, and precise.

Consider the following questions in your reflection:

- How do you currently approach outlining?
- What challenges do you face when outlining your essays?
- Do you find it easy or difficult to organize your thoughts and ideas?
- How do you decide what information to include in your outline?
- What are your strengths when doing this?
- What has worked well when you get stuck?

As students developed their outlines, Mr. Thompson provided ongoing feedback, highlighting strengths and suggesting improvements. He encouraged them to identify strategies to tackle challenges before offering guidance. After submitting their outlines with self-assessments, they received personalized feedback based on a rubric (see Figure 9.3). He also modeled rubric usage and facilitated peer reviews. By focusing on strengths and clear criteria, Mr. Thompson empowered students to take ownership of their learning and enhance their writing skills. See Appendix 11 for an example or a task self-reflection tool.

FIGURE 9.3: MR. THOMPSON'S FEEDBACK RUBRIC

TITLE AND DATE OF OUTLINE	SPECIFIC STRATEGY OR ACTION USED OR APPLIED PRIOR TO MOVING TO ESSAY	TITLE AND DATE OF FINAL ESSAY
Clear Thesis Statement 1 2 3 4		Clear Thesis Statement 1 2 3 4
Logical Organization 1 2 3 4		Logical Organization 1 2 3 4
Effective Use of Evidence 1 2 3 4		Effective Use of Evidence 1 2 3 4
Comprehensive Coverage 1 2 3 4		Comprehensive Coverage 1 2 3 4
Clarity and Conciseness 1 2 3 4		Clarity and Conciseness 1 2 3 4

Mr. Thompson strongly considered, as part of his feedback to and grading of students, their reflection as well as how students *applied* strategies and actions to move their outlines into solid essays. By doing so, he helped students develop assessment capability for future writing tasks that will stand the test of time. Their grades now became much more related to a fluid aspect of learning versus the finality of just an indication of a task being complete.

Reflect and Consider

How can you build in opportunities for your students to self-assess when provided specific criteria? ●

_____

_____

_____

_____

Avoid Early Grading

We've all experienced beginner's luck or early failure, whether in sports or other areas. Early success can lead to frustration when challenges arise, while early failure can cause people to avoid trying again. When students are learning new skills, they need deliberate practice—repetition with feedback to refine their abilities. Learning often comes more from errors than initial success. If students don't fear early mistakes affecting their grades, they develop better assessment skills (Nagel, 2015). Grading too soon on correctness shifts focus from learning strategies to simply earning points (Kluger & DeNisi, 1996).

Training Tasks

A strategy to avoid early grading and promote deliberate practice is using "training tasks." These concise assessments focus on key prerequisite skills needed to advance to deeper learning. Both teachers and students use them to gauge readiness for the next phase or identify areas needing more practice and feedback. The concept is inspired by "training camp" in sports or the military, where early practices focus on fundamentals before competition, with mistakes expected as part of the learning process. The emphasis is on performance and proficiency, not just task completion.

Training Tasks as an Initial Assessment Tool and De-Stressor

Far too often, being judged or graded causes a great deal of stress for students when they are not at a mastery level. In Chapter 10, we will go into more detail about students using feedback and viewing errors as a path to learning. Training tasks are a great precursor to that. Stanford University's Challenge Success program examined responses from over 50,000 high school students asking them what causes them stress and anxiety, and received the following responses:

- 76 percent mentioned not doing well in school
- 75 percent reported being stressed by schoolwork
- 72 percent worry about taking assessments (Feldman, 2020)

A key element of training tasks is that they are not graded in terms of a grade in the grade book. Teachers use evidence from the tasks to know and support students to move on to more complex tasks and concepts. The incentive is not points or a grade but less work and fewer tasks to complete.

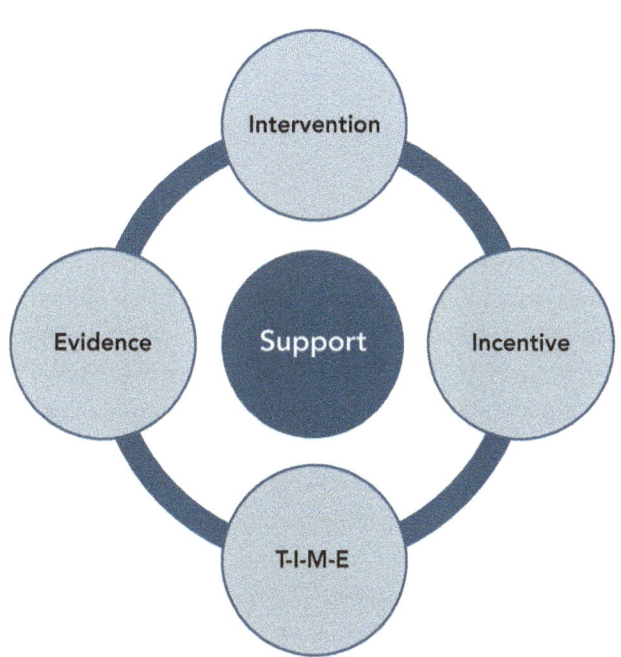

SI²TE Model

*It's important that teachers develop systems of actions to **incentivize** students toward achievement and desired behaviors rather than relying on consequences. Unlike simple rewards, these actions aim to deepen student motivation by fostering a fuller understanding of topics and content, emphasizing the importance of engaging in learning tasks. This approach encourages students to value the learning process itself, leading to intrinsic motivation and sustained academic growth.*

VIGNETTES

Biology Example: Training Task for Multiplication Facts Understanding and Basic Probability

Mr. Jones, a biology teacher at Wonder High School, uses training assignments at the beginning of units to assess students' development of essential math probability skills before progressing to more complex tasks related to genetics and human heredity.

Recognizing the need for deliberate practice, Mr. Jones created two *ungraded training tasks* that provided specific feedback to students below mastery, helping them refine their math skills. Once students showed enough proficiency, they moved on to the first of three larger tasks (tasks 4-5-6). He also introduced a third training task for those needing additional practice in probability.

Mr. Jones implemented mastery grading for all tasks, awarding points only for submissions demonstrating mastery or significant progress. Student work below mastery for tasks 4-5-6 received an "IP" (in progress) grade in the gradebook. Students and parents were informed that feedback could be used for resubmission to improve grades. Additionally, Mr. Jones included a performance target above

(Continued)

(Continued)

mastery for tasks 4, 5 and 6, encouraging students to aim higher (see challenge tasks, Chapter 10).

Social Studies: Understanding Concept of Argument

Mr. Self, a language arts teacher at Wonder Middle School with ten years of experience, uses training tasks to address foundational skills early in the semester. Previously, he often felt frustrated discovering, too late in units, that some students lacked the essential skills needed for challenging material. A major assignment each semester is an argumentative essay, and Mr. Self felt disheartened reading essays with perfect grammar but weak arguments. To tackle this, he introduced training tasks at the beginning of the argumentative essay unit to ensure students understood what constitutes a strong argument and he could identify those needing extra support. Like Mr. Jones, he created two initial training tasks for students to demonstrate their understanding of quality argument elements, along with a third task for those who did not achieve significant progress (SPG) on the first two. He also employed mastery grading for tasks 4-5-6 (see Figures 9.4 and 9.5). •

FIGURE 9.4: EXAMPLES OF TRAINING TASKS

	1	2	3	4	5	6
	Training Task Probability Lab (Coin Flipping)	Training Task Genetic Cross Lab	Optional Training Task (If Not-Proficient on Task 2) Double Trait Cross probability Lab	Heredity Task 50 Points (M) 35 Minimum (SPG)	Genetic Disease Essay 90 Points (E) 80 (M) 70 (SPG)	Summative Performance Assessment Design campaign pro or against pre-birth genetic testing 120 Points (E) 100 (M) 80 (SPG)
Kristen	M+	E	N/A	(M) 50	(E) 90	(M) 100
Brittany	M-	M	N/A	(SPG) 35	(M) 80	(E) 120
Mark	NME	NME	SPG	(SPG) 35	IP Feedback	(SPG) 80
Samantha	SPG	NME	M-	IP Feedback	(SPG) 70	IP-Feedback

Strategy—*Use Training Assignments Early in Units*

E = Exemplary, M = Mastery, SPG = Significant Progress, NME = No Mastery Evidence, IP—In Progress

SOURCE: Adapted from Nagel (2015).

FIGURE 9.5: EXAMPLES OF TRAINING TASK—ELA ARGUMENTATIVE ESSAY

	TRAINING TASK 1 (ARGUMENT ATTRIBUTES)	TRAINING TASK 2 (ARGUMENT ATTRIBUTES)	OPTIONAL TRAINING TASK	ELEMENTS OF EFFECTIVE ARGUMENTATION (M = 50) (SPG = 35)	ARGUMENTATIVE ESSAY (E = 90, M = 80, SPG = 70)	SUMMATIVE PROJECT: ARGUING PRO-AGAINST (E = 120, M = 100, SPG = 80)
Kristen	M+	E	N/A	M (50)	E (90)	M (100)
Brittany	M–	M	N/A	SPG (35)	M (80)	E (120)
Sam	NME	NME	SPG	SPG (35)	IP → Feedback	SPG (80)
Mark	SPG	NME	M–	IP → Feedback	SPG (70)	IP → Feedback

E = exemplary, M = mastery, SPG = significant progress, NME = no mastery evidence, IP = in progress

SOURCE: Adapted from Nagel (2015)

CHAPTER REFLECTION

1. In what ways will you use success criteria to apply accurate scoring of student work?

2. How will you ensure your focus on scoring is framed on the skill or concept, giving the process it's due, while overcoming the commonly held belief that you must grade each task as a separate entity?

3. How can you incorporate the use of training tasks as described in use at Wonder Middle School? ●

NOTES

_____

_____

_____

_____

NOTES

CHAPTER 10

Great Learners Determine How to Seek Feedback and Recognize Errors Are Opportunities to Learn

"Only those who dare to fail greatly can ever achieve greatly."
—Robert Kennedy

 **VIGNETTES**

Steve and Joann are both eighth graders at Anywhere Middle School.

Steve frequently struggles to keep up with his schoolwork and grades, not due to a lack of effort but because he has trouble concentrating in class and managing six subjects. At home, with four siblings, finding a quiet space to study is challenging. Despite this, Steve stays engaged, often attending optional lunch sessions and staying after class for extra help. Both of his parents are successful professionals who excelled academically, as do his siblings, making Steve feel like the odd one out. Recently, he received his report card with the following grades:

(Continued)

(Continued)

SUBJECT	TEACHER	GRADE	EFFORT
Pre-Algebra	Jones	C–	Excellent
8th ELA	A. Bulla	D+	Fair
Physical Education	Smith	A	Excellent
Social Studies	Meenan	C–	Excellent
Science	York	D	Excellent
Band	Fillman	B+	Fair

Steve, as usual around report card time, feels dejected as he goes over his grades with his parents. His mom and dad even noted that "well, he's trying hard, so maybe he's just not strong in these subjects or just not very smart?" Steve feels that no matter what he does he's just not going to do well in school. This mindset was perpetuated with him as he entered high school, where he eventually dropped out.

Joann is very different from Steve. She finds school relatively easy and often puts forth little effort to excel in her classes. Her teachers are often frustrated with her for not accepting additional challenges they come up with in class when she completes required work ahead of schedule and with much more ease than her classmates. Joann thinks that since she is doing "just fine," why would she challenge herself and "risk lowering my grades"? In addition, rarely do teachers seek her input as to what might interest her in terms of additional challenges.

SUBJECT	TEACHER	GRADE	EFFORT
Pre-Algebra	Jones	A–	Needs improvement
8th ELA	A. Bulla	A	Fair
Physical Education	Smith	B–	Excellent
Social Studies	Meenan	B+	Needs improvement
Science	York	A+	Fair
Band	Fillman	A–	Fair

As Joann entered high school, she shied away from taking challenging rigorous classes like honors or advanced placement. She felt that her current level of achievement was linked to the *perception* that her success was due to innate *smartness* and not related to what her potential could be with deep focus on effort. She struggled as she progressed into high school where the course work became more challenging and required her to apply the skills and disposition of being a good learner. ●

Reflect and Consider

What are some reflections related to the scenario related to Steve and Joann?

_____
_____
_____
_____
_____

SUCCESS CRITERIA

As a reader, after reading this chapter, I will be able to

1. Understand that feedback is connected to success criteria and grading
2. Determine the appropriate strategies to use situationally when giving students feedback
3. Understand the volatility of our grading actions—how we can detract from creating environments where errors are seen as opportunities to learn

COMMONLY HELD BELIEFS	COUNTERPOINT
Students won't do work it if it's not graded	Experience often perpetuates this belief and primary teachers rarely encounter this issue. Page's (1958) study and subsequent research demonstrated that specific feedback, rather than just a grade, improves achievement across assessments. R. Butler and Nisan (1986) discovered that providing descriptive feedback, rather than grades, yielded better results in follow-up quantitative tasks and problem-solving assignments. Students who received grades performed better than those who received no feedback on quantitative tasks but not on problem-solving tasks. Overall, evaluative feedback, such as grades, did not improve students' future performance in problem-solving.

(Continued)

(Continued)

COMMONLY HELD BELIEFS	COUNTERPOINT
More grades mean better feedback	We promote the mindset to grade *less*. In addition to the time commitment of grading, learners are inclined to grow from specific and timely (d = 0.89) feedback. Professor Hattie once said, "The simplest prescription for improving education must be dollops of feedback." The more we can be precise in the feedback we deliver to students, the more they are likely to use it and develop ways to provide feedback to themselves.

Report Cards *Can* Lead to Hodgepodge Grading

In Chapter 7, we discussed Tom Guskey's warning about "hodgepodge grading," where final grades often include elements beyond academic achievement, such as collaboration, behavior, participation, and effort (Guskey, 2015a, 2020). Despite its flaws, hodgepodge grading is rarely challenged, as these nonacademic factors are often valued by students, parents, and communities (Guskey & Brookhart, 2019).

Our goal should be to make grading fluid, offering feedback that guides students on their next learning steps. As John Hattie notes, formative feedback is when the chef tastes the soup, and summative feedback is when the customers do. While report cards remain a school tradition, we challenge the system to ensure grades serve as meaningful feedback by 2025, helping students progress in their learning.

Back to Steve and Joann

Providing feedback on students' current achievement levels and future learning steps is crucial for developing visible learners. Guskey and Brookhart caution against including subjective characteristics like effort, attitude, and engagement in report card grades, as these can mislead students. For example, "if the achievement grade is low and the effort grade is high, students may perceive that the effort is not worth it and are less motivated to apply themselves" (Guskey & Brookhart, 2019, p. 78). They also note that separating cognitive and noncognitive grades can convey undesirable messages, such as a student with high achievement but low effort thinking they can excel without effort. To address this, clarity in grading is essential. Aligning grades specifically with academic criteria and learning factors helps ensure feedback is impactful and avoids confusion.

See examples of report cards that reduce hodgepodge grading and allow for more fluidity in learning as well as direction as to where to next in Appendix 12.

Visible Learner Trait and Adult Mindframe Focus for Chapter 10

- **G**auge their current level of understanding.
- **R**eadiness to know where they are going and are confident to take on the challenge.
- **A**dapt tools to guide their learning.
- **D**etermine how to seek and use feedback and recognize that errors are opportunities to learn.
- **E**valuate their progress and adjust their learning.
- Be **S**uccessful in recognizing their learning and teach others.

VISIBLE LEARNERS DETERMINE HOW TO SEEK AND USE FEEDBACK AND RECOGNIZE THAT ERRORS ARE OPPORTUNITIES TO LEARN

To master any skill or concept, learners must seek and use feedback to improve. While feedback is often associated with identifying errors, its real value lies in guiding students on what to do next. Learning is a fluid process, and feedback bridges the gap between where students are and where they need to be. Its main purpose is to enhance the student's ability to perform tasks they haven't yet mastered (Wiliam, 2016).

Feedback ($d = 0.51$) is one of the most powerful of all influences on student learning, but it also has a high level of variability. Teachers need to worry less about how it is delivered and spend much more time and effort monitoring how it is received by their students.

Effective feedback focuses not just on current performance but on how to improve future efforts. This is why success criteria are vital, helping learners seek relevant feedback and self-assess. Grades alone rarely provide useful feedback, especially for problem-solving or creative tasks. Even when grades

(Continued)

(Continued)

include comments, students often don't focus on or act upon them (Schinske & Tanner, 2017).

Embracing errors is key to learning. As Thomas Edison said along his journey to invent the lightbulb, "I have not failed 10,000 times—I've found 10,000 ways that won't work to make a lightbulb!" This mindset is essential for learners to embrace the learning process, including its setbacks. They should view feedback as a tool for improvement, not something punitive. As Brookhart (2008) notes, "It is unfair to give constructive criticism and then use it against students in their grade."

Actions and strategies to support developing learners who seek and use feedback and recognize that errors are opportunities to learn are amnesty days or periods and use of single point rubrics.

Mindframes drive actions to support developing students who can determine how to seek and use feedback and recognize that errors are opportunities to learn.

- I build relationships and trust so that learning can occur in a place where it is safe to make mistakes and learn from others.
- I give and help students understand feedback, and I interpret and act on feedback given to me.

While all mindframes help develop visible learners, two are particularly suited to this student's disposition. It is essential to cultivate an environment where students become their own teachers and view errors as opportunities for learning. Teachers should promote actions that encourage students to seek and use feedback and embrace mistakes rather than impose penalties. Specifically, we need to realize if we want students to embrace a culture of error as a path to learning then we cannot penalize *every* error in gradebooks. Rather, we need to focus actions and approaches instead designed to use feedback to guide further learning.

Aligning effective feedback with grading practices allows students to benefit from feedback without negative grade impacts. When students can draw conclusions from feedback, its effectiveness significantly increases (Harackiewicz, 1979; Harackiewicz et al., 1984). These mindframes prompt teachers to reflect on their influence on student learning and behavior. While life provides many do-overs, they are not infinite and often come with conditions. As we mentioned, we mustn't count every mistake in the grade book, but there should not be an expectation that we don't count any.

VIGNETTES

Scenario 1

As the mid-term period approached in Mr. Ferris's tenth-grade social studies class, he was aware that grades would impact students' eligibility for extracurricular activities, the mid-term honor roll breakfast, and other rewards. As usual, several students struggled to submit assignments on time and had missed classwork. To help, he extended deadlines and offered in-class amnesty periods for students to catch up in the three days leading up to the mid-term deadline. Many students took advantage of this, and most were able to catch up.

However, as the second trimester midterm approached, he found that many of the same students were again behind. Frustrated, Mr. Ferris decided to forgo the amnesty opportunity this time, believing it important for students to learn responsibility. He was disheartened to see a higher number of students falling below passing compared to the first trimester. •

CLASS PERIOD	NUMBER OF STUDENTS BEHIND IN MULTIPLE TASKS/ASSIGNMENTS ONE WEEK BEFORE MIDTERM TRIMESTER 1	NUMBER OF STUDENTS BEHIND IN MULTIPLE TASKS/ASSIGNMENTS AT MIDTERM TRIMESTER 1	NUMBER OF STUDENTS NOT PASSING AFTER MID TERMS	NUMBER OF STUDENTS BEHIND IN MULTIPLE TASKS/ASSIGNMENTS ONE WEEK BEFORE MIDTERM TRIMESTER 2	HOW MANY WERE THE SAME (NEW) STUDENTS FROM TRIMESTER 2?	NUMBER OF STUDENTS NOT PASSING AFTER MID TERMS
1	7/25	1/25	0/25	8/25	7/25	6/25
2	6/28	2/28	1/28	5/28	5/28	4/28
3	9/31	2/31	1/31	9/31	9/31	8/31
4	4/22	0/22	0/22	5/22	4/22	4/22
5	8/23	3/23	2/23	7/23	6/23	5/23
Total	34/129	7/129	**4/129**	34/129	31/129	**27/129**

CHAPTER 10 • GREAT LEARNERS DETERMINE HOW TO SEEK FEEDBACK

STIPULATED SECOND CHANCES

Scenario 2

Mrs. Chick, a ninth-grade algebra teacher at the same school as Mr. Ferris, also faced challenges with students missing deadlines. As midterms approached, she implemented strategies similar to his. A week before midterms, she allocated half a class period for students to complete assignments or seek help. Recognizing that this might not be sufficient for all, she offered a second chance by making herself available after school and during lunch for two days. This approach allowed her to provide valuable feedback and extensions of learning time while emphasizing that this opportunity was contingent on students' personal commitment, particularly for those prone to procrastination.

CLASS PERIOD	NUMBER OF STUDENTS BEHIND IN MULTIPLE TASKS/ ASSIGNMENTS ONE WEEK BEFORE MIDTERM TRIMESTER 1	NUMBER OF STUDENTS BEHIND IN MULTIPLE TASKS ASSIGNMENTS AT MIDTERM TRIMESTER 1	NUMBER OF STUDENTS NOT PASSING AFTER MID TERMS	NUMBER OF STUDENTS BEHIND IN MULTIPLE TASKS/ ASSIGNMENTS ONE WEEK BEFORE MIDTERM TRIMESTER 2	HOW MANY WERE THE SAME (NEW) STUDENTS FROM TRIMESTER 2?	NUMBER OF STUDENTS NOT PASSING AFTER MIDTERMS OF TRIMESTER 2
2	10/23	4/23	2/23	5/23	2/23	1/23
3	7/21	2/21	2/21	3/21	2/21	2/21
4	8/29	3/29	1/29	3/29	2/29	1/29
5	6/26	2/26	1/26	2/26	1/26	1/26
6	7/20	3/20	3/20	3/20	2/20	2/20
Total	38/119	14/129	**11/119**	16/129	8/129	**7/129**

While there were some of the same students who were behind at the midterm of Trimesters 1 and 2, there were *fewer, and her overall failure rate was continuing to decrease.* Mrs. Chick shared this with her professional learning community (PLC) team, and several colleagues replicated the practice the following year with similar successes as hers.

REFLECT AND CONSIDER

Based on the previous scenarios, how will you monitor the impact of stipulated second chances?

_____
_____
_____
_____

COMMONLY HELD GRADING BELIEFS	COUNTERPOINT
Students won't do work it if it's not graded.	Experience often perpetuates this belief and primary teachers rarely encounter this issue. Page's (1958) landmark study demonstrated that specific feedback, rather than just a grade, or even a grade with prespecified comments, improved achievement over time and across assessments. Subsequent research studies have also supported this (D. L. Butler & Winne, 1995; Carless, 2006; Kluger & DiNisi, 1996).
More grades mean better feedback.	We promote the mindset to grade less. In addition to the time commitment of grading, learners are inclined to grow from specific and timely ($d = 0.89$) feedback. Professor Hattie once said: "The simplest prescription for improving education must be dollops of feedback." The more we can be precise in the feedback we deliver to students, the more they are likely to use it and develop ways to provide feedback to themselves.

Feedback Should Align With, Not Oppose Grading Actions

We all *know* feedback is important for learning, but unpacking how feedback can work best to increase learning has long been the challenge. Feedback has shown to have a high effect size but has also shown to be one of the most variable of all of Hattie's visible learning influences. For example, if we provide students feedback today it's effective, and if we provide the exact same feedback tomorrow it may not be. Why? That's the question researchers have been trying to uncover for some time. A simple way to think about it is you could provide a colleague or another adult feedback right now and it's very effective for helping them. You provide them the *exact same* feedback fifteen minutes from now and it's not. Why? . . . Because of a text message *they just read!* Hattie defines feedback ($d = 0.51$) as information provided by an agent (e.g., teacher, peer, book, parent, self/experience) regarding aspects of one's performance or understanding that reduces the discrepancy between what is understood, what is aimed to be understood, and where to move next in their learning (Visiblelearningmetax.com; see Figure 10.1).

> The evolution of examining research on feedback has brought us to some important things to consider in 2025 and beyond.
>
> 1. Feedback is multi-dimensional and cannot be treated as a one dimensional concept
> 2. There are now different aspects of feedback (See Fig 10.1) and having a singular view of feedback as one construct is not sufficient to move student learning forward
> 3. There is a great deal of variation related to feedback and educators need to be aware of these
> 4. Understanding how feedback drives learning is essential as teachers navigate how to best utilize its potential as well as supporting students in doing so to become visible learners

SOURCE: Adapted from Almarode et al. (2022).

FIGURE 10.1: EFFECT SIZE BY FEEDBACK TYPE

Feedback from tasks and process (d = 0.61)
Feedback timing (d = 0.89)
Feedback from tests (d = 0.41)
(Tying to) Student Emotions (d = .061)
Feedback from reinforcement/cues (d = 1.01)

SOURCE: Visiblelearningmetax.com.

In Hattie's latest iteration related to the impact of feedback on learning, he broke down different aspects of feedback. When he published the original *Visible Learning* research in 2009, feedback had an effect size of 0.73 (p. 173). This included all aspects and studies related to feedback. In 2024, there were 37 meta-analyses made up of 1,620 studies that helped us differentiate different variations of feedback and their impact on student learning. Grading actions and practices must be aligned with and viewed through the lens of effective feedback. We can also look at how we break feedback down into different aspects of classroom practice.

We develop stronger learners when we teach students that the role of feedback is to reinforce something they have done well and to replicate that versus just to fix errors or mistakes they have made. Bruce and I periodically conduct visible learning school capability assessments. The process involves surveying staff members and then an on-site visit to the school that involves classroom observations and student focus group interviews. We ask students from kindergarten up through twelfth grade questions about how they view themselves as learners, how their school and teachers are helping them develop as quality learners, and so on. One of the questions we ask students is "What is feedback, and how do they use feedback to learn." Conducting over forty of these, we have interviewed over 800 students. We tallied the number of students' responses in Figure 10.2 to this question:

FIGURE 10.2: STUDENTS' RESPONSES TO THE QUESTION "WHAT IS FEEDBACK?"

Something that is provided to you to tell you what you did **wrong** and how to fix it	Something that is provided to you to tell you what you did **right** and to do it again	Both something that is about what you have done **right as well as what you have done wrong**
65%	8%	27%

The key to developing students who seek and use feedback to guide their learning and value errors as a learning opportunity is ensuring they understand both are essential. We noted previously the impact of feedback from *reinforcement and cues (d = 1.01)*. It's critical that students are aware that the learning path they are on is the right one, because if not, they are likely to drift away from it into behaviors that are random or not aligned. Reinforcing behaviors strengthens the connections students make with what they are doing with the cue provided to them, thus increasing the likelihood of continuing or repeating the behavior (Dollard & Miller, 1950).

CORE PRACTICE

At Wonder Intermediate School, teachers initially gathered to calibrate their grading but shifted their focus to providing effective feedback after Lisa proposed a new approach. Instead of just scoring, they decided to concentrate on offering constructive feedback that would guide student improvement. They reviewed student papers collectively, with each teacher providing feedback aligned with the success criteria.

The team began by anonymizing a piece of student work and sharing feedback based on it. Despite some initial disagreements, such as Bill's concern about organization and Alex's praise for writing style, they ultimately aligned on feedback by referencing the success criteria. They repeated this process with several papers to ensure consistency in their feedback.

The respectful dialogue and shared goal of improving student outcomes led the team to agree on making this collaborative feedback review a monthly practice, embracing the opportunity to learn from each other and enhance their teaching effectiveness.

> **REFLECT AND CONSIDER**
>
> How could providing collaborative feedback increase the quality of feedback teachers and teams provide students?
>
> _____
> _____
> _____
> _____
> _____

Single Point Rubrics

Brookhart (2008, p. 8) concludes, "the grade trumps the comment and comments have the best chance of being *read* as descriptive if they are not accompanied by a grade." The more feedback is specific and precise to what the learner must consider for their next learning step, the more it is likely to be used. We therefore advocate the use of single point rubrics.

The use of single point rubrics (SPRs) is a strategy that provides clear expectations and success criteria for assignments, tasks, performances, and so on, while allowing for flexibility and personalized feedback (see Figure 10.3). SPRs also

FIGURE 10.3: SINGLE POINT RUBRIC

FEEDBACK TO IMPROVE YOUR WORK TOWARD PROFICIENCY OR MASTERY	SUCCESS CRITERIA (DESCRIPTION OF PRODUCT OR PERFORMANCE AT PROFICIENT OR MASTERY LEVEL)	STRONG ASPECTS OF YOUR WORK TO REPLICATE NEXT TIME OR IDEAS ENHANCE YOUR WORK FURTHER TO GO TO NEXT LEVEL

simplify the grading process for teachers and help students focus on specific areas for improvement (see Figure 10.4). Additionally, they emphasize progress toward mastery as well as what the student's next learning step is. Instead of cumbersome overly wordy criteria for what a lack of proficiency would look like, single point rubrics focus learners' attention on meeting *one* level of success at a time and using *feedback* to examine how they are making progress and what their next learning step should be.

Standard: 3.NF.3. Explain equivalence of fractions in special cases, and compare fractions by reasoning about their size

FIGURE 10.4: THIRD-GRADE MATH EXAMPLE

GROW FEEDBACK TO IMPROVE YOUR WORK TOWARD PROFICIENCY OR MASTERY	SUCCESS CRITERIA I CAN . . .	GLOW STRONG ASPECTS OF YOUR WORK TO REPLICATE NEXT TIME OR IDEAS ENHANCE YOUR WORK FURTHER TO GO TO NEXT LEVEL
	#1 Model fractions of a whole quantity, length, shape, or object in various ways limited to denominators of 12 or less	
	#2 Visualize fractions as compositions of a unit fraction	
	#3 Identify the numerator and denominator of a fraction in various representations	

(Continued)

(Continued)

GROW FEEDBACK TO IMPROVE YOUR WORK TOWARD PROFICIENCY OR MASTERY	SUCCESS CRITERIA I CAN . . .	GLOW STRONG ASPECTS OF YOUR WORK TO REPLICATE NEXT TIME OR IDEAS ENHANCE YOUR WORK FURTHER TO GO TO NEXT LEVEL
_____ _____ _____ _____ _____	#4 Name a given fraction	_____ _____ _____ _____ _____
_____ _____ _____ _____ _____	#5 Express fractions including one whole symbolically limited to denominators of 12 or less	_____ _____ _____ _____ _____
_____ _____ _____ _____ _____	#6 Relate various representations of the same fraction limited to denominators of 12 or less	_____ _____ _____ _____ _____
_____ _____ _____ _____ _____	#7 Compare the same fraction of different sized wholes	_____ _____ _____ _____ _____
_____ _____ _____ _____ _____	#8 Compare different fractions of the same whole that have the same denominator	_____ _____ _____ _____ _____

# VIGNETTES

At Wonder Elementary School, the third-grade team gathered around a table covered with math manipulatives and fraction charts to discuss their new approach to teaching fractions using a single point rubric.

Ms. Baker, who enjoyed making math engaging, led the discussion. "The single point rubric is great for focusing on core objectives while allowing specific feedback."

Mr. Evans, enthusiastic about new strategies, agreed. "Yes, especially for modeling fractions. We need students to represent fractions in various ways—objects, drawings, or number lines—with denominators up to 12."

Ms. Chen, with insights from higher grades, added, "Looking ahead to fourth grade, where they dive into fraction addition, subtraction, and equivalents, our feedback now will set a strong foundation."

"Exactly," said Ms. Lopez, known for her detailed feedback. "We'll highlight when students accurately model fractions and use correct notation, and clarify concepts like 3/4 being three out of four parts."

Ms. Baker suggested, "We can praise students who use multiple methods to represent fractions, like drawings and fraction strips, to show their understanding and prepare them for equivalent fractions."

Mr. Evans added, "For students who grasp concepts well, we can introduce simple equivalent fractions, like 1/2 equals 2/4, giving them a head start."

Ms. Chen agreed, "Encouraging explanations in writing will be crucial as they move to more complex operations in fourth grade."

By the end of the meeting, the team felt confident and excited to implement their single point rubric, focusing on solidifying fraction skills and providing feedback that prepared students for future learning.

Feedback Doesn't Know if It's Practice or a Game

Teachers and PLC teams often debate whether assessments are formative or summative when determining how to use evidence from them and their impact on grades. As Bruce and I completed our manuscript's first draft, we sought extensive peer reviews, hoping for positive affirmations as well as constructive criticism, particularly from current practitioners, to enhance our work. We received both, aiding us in refining the manuscript.

A key piece of critical feedback from one reviewer was the assertion that "formative assessment information *should never* contribute to a grade." While we understand this perspective, we reject the all-or-nothing view. Take, for example, a high school football player refining their routes and catching techniques in practice. Feedback from the coach during practice on Tuesday or Wednesday is *just as impactful for learning* as feedback received during a Friday night game; the setting shouldn't always dictate or be a sole determining factor in its value.

Of course, some practice opportunities may not factor into final assessments of learning, we need to reconsider the belief that meaningful feedback and true assessment can *only* happen during evaluations like games or tests.

While final evaluation of products or performance will always be a key in determining course grades, they should never be based solely on work that rewards only correct answers, such as exams and quizzes. Evidence shows that when teachers and teams construct grading systems that recognize and reward students for participation and effort, it has been shown to stimulate student interest in improvement (Swinton, 2010). We must view feedback through both evaluative and descriptive lenses:

- Evaluative feedback: Letter grades or written praise or criticism that judges student work against specific criteria

- Descriptive feedback: Provides advice for how students can become more competent

(Brookhart, 2008, p. 26)

We advocate for the use of single point rubrics to focus students on specific criteria to seek feedback and use errors as a path to learning. However, SPRs will be useless for students unless the feedback provides them evidence for where they are making progress and where to go next in their learning. Descriptive, written feedback enhances student performance across the board, especially on problem-solving tasks; (Crisp, 2007; MacDonald, 1991). Reaping the benefits of learning and thus the benefits of SPRs requires students to read, understand, and use the feedback. Sometimes, teachers and PLC teams need to reconsider what some potential feedback would be for students who fall short or who need to be challenged to move past the established level of success criteria. See Appendix 13 for a sample Collaborative Feedback Tool.

VIGNETTES

Revisiting Wonder Elementary's Third-Grade Team Using a Slightly Different Lens

At Wonder Elementary School, the third-grade team met to plan their new math unit on fractions, using a single point rubric to focus their feedback and scoring and to identify areas for improvement.

Ms. Baker, excited about the new approach, started the meeting. "I'm thrilled about using the single point rubric. It'll help us concentrate on key objectives and provide specific feedback."

Mr. Evans, eager to share his thoughts, agreed. "Yes, we need to ensure students can model fractions with various denominators up to 12 and express them symbolically."

Ms. Chen, with her broader perspective, suggested, "For 'Grows,' we should give feedback that guides further learning. If a student struggles with shapes, we could recommend more practice with fraction circles or rectangles."

Ms. Lopez, known for her detailed feedback, added, "We should also praise their efforts. If a student models a fraction but the parts are slightly uneven, we should encourage their attempt while guiding them to improve precision."

Ms. Baker proposed, "For instance, if a student shows $\frac{3}{4}$ with fraction strips but struggles with drawing it, we could say, 'Great job with the strips! Now, let's practice drawing it.'"

Mr. Evans suggested, "For symbolic representation, if a student writes $\frac{4}{6}$ but doesn't grasp it represents four parts out of six, we could offer feedback like, 'You've written $\frac{4}{6}$ correctly. Let's explore what this looks like with shapes or on a number line.'"

Ms. Chen added, "We should also introduce concepts they'll encounter in fourth grade, such as equivalent fractions. Showing that $\frac{4}{6}$ equals $\frac{2}{3}$ can extend their understanding."

Ms. Lopez concluded, "The focus should be on their strengths while guiding improvements. Praising effort and perseverance is crucial for their growth and confidence."

As the meeting ended, the team felt ready and motivated, equipped with their single point rubric and a strategic approach to feedback to help their students master fractions effectively.

In Figure 10.5, see a sample modified rubric with three different scenarios putting this theory into practice.

FIGURE 10.5: CGSG FEEDBACK/FEEDFORWARD MODEL

CONCEPT	#1 MODEL FRACTIONS OF A WHOLE QUANTITY, LENGTH, SHAPE, OR OBJECT IN VARIOUS WAYS LIMITED TO DENOMINATORS OF 12 OR LESS.		
LEARNING STATUS	GROWING	PROFICIENT	ADVANCED
Application Status	The student correctly models 3/4 using fraction strips but struggles with drawing it.	The student effectively models fractions using multiple methods, demonstrating a strong understanding despite minor errors.	The student accurately models fractions with various methods, showing a deep understanding and precise work, and clearly explains their reasoning.
Feedback Status	*Great job using fraction strips to show 3/4! Now let's practice drawing it. I'll give you some extra practice tasks to help with the concept you're struggling with—your perseverance will pay off!*	*Double-check your work for accuracy and practice detailed explanations to strengthen your understanding. You're on the right track—your effort is evident. Keep challenging yourself, and you'll master even the most complex fraction concepts!*	*Your advanced fraction skills are impressive. Continue exploring complex topics and applications. Your dedication is evident, and you're on track to mastering fractions. Consider explaining these concepts to peers to reinforce your understanding and assist others.*
Grade Status	In Progress	3 out of 4 or B	4 out of 4 or A

See Appendix 14 for CGSG With Generative Learning Examples

Going Deeper With Feedback

We noted above that developing learners who seek and *use* feedback means we need to help students be *more active in using* the feedback we provide them. The agreement in the research is that there are four types of feedback (Hattie & Timperley, 2007):

1. Task
2. Process
3. Self-Regulation
4. Self-Praise

The first three are considered part of the instructional model for feedback (see Figure 10.6). We provide task feedback when learners are new or emergent, and this type of feedback is usually related to accuracy or correct or incorrect responses. We should use process feedback when learners are developing proficiency, and we are attempting to provide the right kind of cues and reinforcement to help them detect errors and best determine what strategies to apply. Self-regulation feedback guides learners when they have reached deeper levels of conceptual understanding and are ready to self-regulate on their own. Here the main role of the teacher is to ask questions to prompt students to use metacognition, self-verbalization, self-questioning, and self-reflection (Fisher et al., 2024).

FIGURE 10.6: HATTIE AND TIMPERLEY FEEDBACK MODEL (2007)

TYPE OF FEEDBACK	CONSIDERATIONS	WHEN TO APPLY
Task	How well has a task been performed; is the information correct or incorrect?	New Material—Emergent Learner
Process	What are the strategies needed to perform the task; are there alternative strategies that can be used?	When there is some degree of proficiency
Self-Regulation	Self-Monitoring to achieve a goal	When there is a high degree of proficiency

When integrating the different types of feedback in situational contexts the common thread for the impact is always how feedback is aligned to *clarity*.

> Clarity is an essential part of making feedback work. By having answers to the three questions—what, why, and how—we have insight into the substance of the feedback given, received, and integrated. The content of the feedback exchanged in our schools and classrooms should move us forward in the learning progression. However, if that learning progression and the steps within that progression are not clearly defined, feedback can turn into empty statements."
>
> (Almarode et al., 2022)

# VIGNETTES

Back at Wonder High School, the three-member business department gathered for their weekly meeting to discuss the agenda topic, Formation of Legal Systems Unit for their Business Law class.

Mr. Johnson (department head): "Today, let's focus on giving effective feedback about understanding laws and their purposes. Ensure our feedback encourages a growth mindset."

Ms. Shoei: "We should target specific elements of the assignments. For example, if a student defines what a law is but doesn't explain why we have laws, we can say, 'You defined a law well. Now, explain its purpose to complete your answer.' This helps them see their strengths and areas for improvement."

Mr. Green: "For process feedback, suggest steps for deeper understanding, like, 'Research historical examples of laws to better explain their purpose.' This guides them to improve their approach and shows that learning is ongoing."

Ms. Shoei: "Yes, and for process feedback, suggest organizing their thoughts before writing. For instance, 'Outline your answer to ensure you cover all parts of the question.' This helps them view mistakes as learning opportunities."

Mr. Johnson: "For self-regulation feedback, encourage reflection on their work. For example, 'You defined a law well. Now, ask if your explanation of why we have laws is as clear. How can you improve it?' This promotes self-monitoring and sees errors as learning chances."

Mr. Green: "Combining all types of feedback could be effective. For example, 'You defined a law well (Task). Look at historical examples for better explanation (Process). Reflect on your explanation's clarity and ways to improve (Self-Regulation).' This gives comprehensive feedback and reassures them that failure is part of learning."

Ms. Shoei: "I agree. Balancing specific, constructive, and encouraging feedback while emphasizing strengths will keep students motivated."

Mr. Johnson: "Perfect. Let's ensure our feedback is balanced and reinforces that mistakes are part of learning. We want our students to embrace challenges and grow both academically and personally."

The team concluded the meeting, ready to guide students through understanding the Formation of Legal Systems with feedback that supports their learning process effectively.

See the CGSG in Figure 10.7 clearly identifying where the appropriate use of feedback is required to move learning forward.

FIGURE 10.7: CLARITY OF GRADING SCORING GUIDE (CGSG)

Mindframes for Learning: Which Is a Focus for This Unit/Lesson	*Visible Learner Trait*
I give and help students understand feedback, and I interpret and act on feedback given to me. I build relationships and trust so that learning can occur in a place where it is safe to make mistakes and learn from others.	**Determine** feedback and recognize that errors are opportunities to learn

	GENERATIVE LEARNING EXPERIENCES	WEIGHTED SCORING
SURFACE	**TASK FEEDBACK—Understanding the Differences Between Common Law and Positive Law** **Objective:** To help students recall, retrieve, and memorize key information about how common law differs from positive law. Task 1: Vocabulary Matching Task 2: Fill-in-the-Blanks Fill in the blanks with the appropriate term from the list: (common law, positive law, precedent, statute) Task 3: Comparison Chart Complete the following comparison chart by listing at least two key characteristics for each type of law.	0.5X
	PROCESS FEEDBACK—Understanding and Processing the Differences Between Common Law and Positive Law **Objective:** To help students understand and process the key differences between common law and positive law through analysis, discussion, and Task 1: Concept Mapping Create a concept map that illustrates the differences between common law and positive law. Task 2: Case Study Analysis Read the following case studies, and identify whether they pertain to common law or positive law. Explain your reasoning. Task 3: Group Discussion In small groups, discuss the following questions, and be prepared to share your thoughts with the class. Task 4: Comparative Essay Write a short essay (300–400 words) comparing and contrasting common law and positive law.	X
	PRECIPICE OF COGNITIVE CHALLENGE	
DEEP	**SELF REGULATION FEEDBACK—Analyzing, and Linking Information on Common Law vs. Positive Law** **Objective:** To help students apply, analyze, and link information to understand the differences between common law and positive law. Task 1: Application in Real-Life Scenarios Consider the following real-life scenarios, and determine whether they involve common law or positive law. Explain your reasoning and discuss the implications of each system's application.	1.5X

(Continued)

(Continued)

PRECIPICE OF COGNITIVE CHALLENGE	
Task 2: Case Analysis Read the following case summaries, and analyze how common law and positive law are applied. Answer the questions that follow each case. Task 3: Linking Concepts Create a Venn diagram that compares and contrasts common law and positive law. Include the following elements: Common Law Characteristics: Based on judicial decisions and legal precedents Evolves through interpretation by courts Flexible and adaptable to unique cases Examples: Tort law, contract law (in common law jurisdictions) Positive Law Characteristics: Established through formal legislation or codification Enacted by a recognized authority (e.g., government or legislature) Provides clear, uniform rules Examples: Criminal law, regulatory statutes Task 4: Analytical Essay Write an analytical essay (400-500 words) on the topic: "The Interplay Between Common Law and Positive Law in Modern Legal Systems."	

| TRANSFER | **SELF REGULATION FEEDBACK-Understanding the Differences Between Common Law and Positive Law**

Objective: To analyze and distinguish between common law and positive law, evaluating their key characteristics and legal implications.

1. **Research Phase:**
   - **Evaluate:** Conduct research to understand the fundamental principles and origins of common law and positive law.
   - **Compare:** Identify and compare the historical development and theoretical foundations of common law and positive law.

2. **Argumentation Phase:**
   - **Argue:** Formulate arguments for and against the effectiveness and adaptability of common law and positive law in modern legal systems.
   - **Defend:** Defend your chosen legal system (common law or positive law) by articulating its strengths in ensuring justice and consistency.

3. **Justification Phase:**
   - **Justify:** Provide reasoned justifications for why certain legal jurisdictions predominantly follow common law or positive law principles.
   - **Information Gathering:** Gather relevant case studies or examples to illustrate how common law and positive law are applied in different legal contexts.

4. **Presentation:**
   - Prepare a presentation or report summarizing your findings and arguments.
   - Present your conclusions on how common law and positive law differ in their approach to legal reasoning and application. | 2X |

CHAPTER REFLECTION

1. How will you use feedback so that it's connected to feedback and grading?
2. Which strategies can you implement to maximize the impact of your feedback to students?
3. What guard rails will you put into place to avoid actions that detract from creating an environment where errors are opportunities to learn?

NOTES

NOTES

CHAPTER 11

Great Learners Evaluate Their Progress

"We learn from failure, not from success!"

—Bram Stoker

Opening Prose

Parents often ask their children, "How did you get that grade?" to which many respond, "I don't know!" This isn't always dishonesty; grading and feedback can be confusing. Unlike twenty years ago, when final grades were posted only at the end of a term, today's schools use electronic systems for real-time grade access. While this convenience helps parents and students track learning status, it hasn't improved students' understanding of how grades are determined or their significance for future learning.

The following are responses from 500+ students (Grades 5–12) being asked, "How did you get the grade you did?":

RESPONSE	#/% OF RESPONSES FROM 500 STUDENTS
I don't know	385 (77%)
The teacher (did or did not) like me	55 (11%)
That's what I earned	40 (8%)
Other	20 (4%)

SUCCESS CRITERIA

As a reader, after reading this chapter, I will be able to

1. Determine actions to minimize student perfectionism
2. Determine ways to limit student frustration in their learning
3. Determine the most effective ways to use homework and practice
4. Determine how to use the concept of amnesty days to promote achievement and student ownership
5. Use the concept of missing essential assignments or assessments extended chances (MEAECs) to help students better determine learning progress

VIGNETTES

Rod Fralinger, the enigmatic sociology teacher at Anywhere High School, is popular and relates well to high school students. He is well liked as his actions and classroom antics demonstrate dynamism in his teaching. On test days, Rod wears sunglasses and rarely talks as his tests take up the majority of the class period. He walks in the school with a briefcase handcuffed to him (the tests are in the briefcase). This is to convey that he and only he knows what will be on the test(s), and no one else will know until they crack them open. This adds to his persona.

Rod exudes an aura of mystery when it comes to his grading practices. Firmly rooted in old-school teaching methods, Rod believes that memorization of definitions, facts, and concepts is the cornerstone of a comprehensive understanding of sociology. However, his cryptic approach to grading leaves some students feeling frustrated and uncertain of how their efforts will be evaluated. Some students have publicly said they avoid signing up for his course even though they have heard how much fun it is, because they worry about not being aware of his grading practices and how this could impact their grade point average (GPA).

While some students thrive on the challenge of deciphering Rod's assessments, others struggle with the lack of clarity. Despite the confusion, Rod's students develop resilience, analytical skills, and independent thinking abilities as they navigate through uncertain circumstances. They learn to adapt to ambiguity, preparing them for real-world challenges outside of the classroom. However, the nebulousness of Rod's grading practices can hinder some students' personal growth, leading them to believe that success is based on luck rather than mastery of content. One student described Rod's grading practices as that of a Ouija board.

In conclusion, Rod Fralinger's popularity among students stems from his engaging teaching style, but his ambiguous grading techniques present both challenges and opportunities for personal growth and learning.

REFLECT AND CONSIDER

How well do your students understand how their grades are determined?

_____
_____
_____
_____
_____

Visible Learner Trait and Adult Mindframe Focus for Chapter 11

- **G**auge their current level of understanding.
- **R**eadiness to know where they are going and are confident to take on the challenge.
- **A**dapt tools to guide their learning.
- **D**etermine feedback and recognize that errors are opportunities to learn.
- **E**valuate their progress and adjust their learning.
- Be **S**uccessful in recognizing their learning and teach others.

VISIBLE LEARNERS CAN EVALUATE THEIR PROGRESS AND ADJUST THEIR LEARNING

Students enhance their learning by actively evaluating their progress and making necessary adjustments. Teachers can facilitate this process by helping students set specific, measurable goals with clear objectives and consistently tracking their progress. Alongside goal setting, students should review their work and seek feedback from teachers and peers. Reflecting on assignments allows them to identify strengths and areas for growth. As noted in Chapter 8, those who actively seek and use feedback gain valuable insights that help refine their learning strategies.

Self-assessment and self-questioning are vital for evaluating progress. By comparing their work to established criteria, students can pinpoint areas for improvement and set new targets. This fosters ownership of their learning and encourages self-direction as they assess their readiness for more complex challenges. Teachers should guide students in seeking help, teaching them to view educators as valuable resources while using supplemental materials and organizing their tasks. Moreover, students must manage challenges like frustration and perfectionism while developing effective study habits, time management skills, and a structured study routine. Prioritizing tasks and allocating time based on challenge levels is essential for success.

The following are specific practices and actions that promote the trait of students being able to evaluate their progress and adjust their learning:

1. Effective use of and monitoring the impact of homework and classwork
2. Use of amnesty days and periods
3. Ensuring students focus on the most important and essential tasks needed for their next step in learning, something we call MEAECs. ●

Mindframes drive actions to support developing students who can evaluate their progress and adjust their learning.

1. I engage as much in dialogue as monologue.
2. I focus on learning and the language of learning

For students to evaluate and adjust their learning, teachers must clearly define what success looks like from the start and communicate it effectively. Without a clear destination, achieving learning goals becomes challenging. Additionally, timely adjustments in teaching are essential for guiding learners along their path.

Establishing clarity about success and creating a shared language around learning among teachers, students, and parents is vital. Communicating what successful learning entails and how it will be assessed is essential. Encouraging students to reflect on their progress and adjust their learning strategies is key to linking this learner trait to the mindframe.

COMMONLY HELD BELIEFS	COUNTERPOINT
All students must have the same assignments to be fair.	While it seems fair, having each student always work on the same task would never allow for differentiation and individual skill development. At the same time having students *all* working on different assignments is not at all practical or even aligned with common curricular goals. Aligning tasks to students' readiness levels and giving them ownership is a more effective way to ensure feedback on learning is impactful.
Punishing students with low grades for missing deadlines teaches responsibility.	Punishing students with lower grades for missing deadlines discourages risk taking and creativity, fostering a fear of failure rather than teaching responsibility. Guskey (2009, 2015b, 2020) has noted several times that punishing students with lower grades has not proved to increase achievement or desired behaviors.

Potential Pitfalls

A mantra to live by (as we have mentioned) is *amateurs react and repair, professionals prepare and prevent!* As teachers and teams engage in planning to support their students in evaluating their progress and making the right adjustments, it is critically important to not allow aspects of grading to derail their efforts. Two important factors to address when planning for instruction and assessment are student frustration and perfectionism.

Frustration

We all understand the feeling of being frustrated. Frustration ($d = -0.04$) is a mix of anger and disappointment that can hinder learning by creating uncertainty about next steps, rather than merely arising from mastery challenges. It impairs cognitive functioning, causing overload and making it difficult to process new information, leading to confusion, anxiety, and self-doubt. While some may build resilience by overcoming frustration, those who fear failure and lack coping strategies may struggle significantly more. Frustration reduces motivation, disengages students from learning, and impedes the development of metacognitive skills. Educators should promote a growth mindset, encourage perseverance, and provide resources to help students manage frustration and remain engaged in their learning journey.

VIGNETTES

In Mrs. Rodriguez's seventh-grade science class at Anywhere Middle School, Alex was an enthusiastic student eager to learn about the natural world. However, he struggled to keep up with the class pace and found complex scientific concepts, like mitosis, particularly challenging. Mrs. Rodriguez did not share learning intentions or success criteria, believing it would spoil the learning process. This lack of clarity left Alex frustrated and confused about the intricacies of cell division.

During discussions and lab activities, Alex hesitated to ask questions, fearing judgment from classmates. Instead, he quietly struggled, feeling increasingly isolated and discouraged. As the unit progressed, his motivation dwindled, and he withdrew from participation and assignments, convinced he couldn't grasp the material.

Outside of class, Alex's frustration affected his study habits and self-esteem. Despite spending hours trying to understand the material, he made little progress, leading to declining grades and a belief that he was not suited for science. Concerned, Mrs. Rodriguez reached out to the special education department chair to consider the possibility of a learning disability. •

REFLECT AND CONSIDER

Does this scenario compare to any experiences of students you know? •

_____
_____
_____
_____

> ## Clarity as a Driver to Minimize Frustration—*Receiver Apprehension*
>
> To develop students who drive their own learning calls for us to teach students to *know what to do when they don't know what to do*. One of the biggest drivers of learner frustration is when they have no idea what to do or how to move forward in their learning. This leads to feelings of helplessness and immobilization, often stemming from what is called *receiver apprehension*.
>
> Wheeless (1975) originally defined *receiver apprehension* (RA) as a fear of misinterpreting, inadequately processing, or struggling to adapt or adjust psychologically to messages sent by others" (p. 263). The idea was expounded on by researchers examining anxiety related to speaking and reading. Chesebro and McCroskey (1999) noted how having (teacher) clarity related to what the goal or focus of the lesson was increased student motivation to learn and increased positive affect and cognitive function toward learning.
>
> The more learners are acutely aware of learning goals as well as possible steps they should take to be able to reach them, the more the receiver apprehension and thus anxiety and frustration toward learning are minimized.

Perfectionism

Perfectionism (d = 0.03) can lead students to set unattainable performance standards, often fueled by a fear of failure or a need for external validation. This relentless pursuit heightens stress, anxiety, and self-doubt, eroding confidence and well-being. Perfectionism encourages a fixed mindset, causing students to equate their self-worth with flawless outcomes and avoid risks or mistakes.

We must avoid overvaluing perfect scores; consistently achieving 100 percent can be detrimental to education. At the 2024 commencement, Bruce's son's valedictorian shared her struggle with perfectionism, confessing it led her to prioritize grades over pursuing genuinely interesting classes, which she now regrets.

Perfectionism undermines adaptability and resilience, as students concentrate on avoiding failure rather than learning from setbacks. This rigidity hampers problem solving and perseverance. While goal setting enhances motivation and self-efficacy, the pursuit of perfection can harm well-being and learning outcomes. Educators should create supportive environments that promote realistic goals, embrace challenges, and view mistakes as growth opportunities.

VIGNETTES

In Mrs. Smith's fourth-grade classroom at Anywhere Elementary School, students sat hunched over their desks, obsessively erasing and rewriting their work. The unspoken rule was that every assignment, test, and project had to be perfect.

Once eager and enthusiastic, many children had become shadows of their former selves. They rarely raised their hands or volunteered to participate. Instead, whispers of anxiety filled the room as they lamented their mistakes. The looming fear of failure stifled their curiosity and discouraged any risks in their learning.

While Mrs. Smith maintained high expectations, her strict grading policy perpetuated a cycle of perfectionism. She frequently praised only those with perfect scores, dismissing mistakes as a lack of effort. Her feedback often criticized what she called "silly mistakes" instead of offering constructive guidance. This led many students to fear disappointing her, with only perfect papers displayed on her success wall.

One day, Tommy, a bright and humorous student, cracked under the pressure of a vocabulary quiz. Tears streamed down his face as he submitted his paper, knowing he hadn't performed well. "I'm sorry, Mrs. Smith, I'll do better next time," he said.

Mrs. Smith was shocked by Tommy's distress and realized she had created an environment where only perfection was acceptable. Mistakes were punished, rather than viewed as growth opportunities. Recognizing the need for change, she contemplated how to shift her students' perceptions. ●

Actions to Promote Students Monitoring Progress

As we have noted, developing *visible learners* starts with *visible teachers* implementing strategies, actions, and approaches to support students. The following are three grading and feedback actions that directly support students in evaluating progress and adjust their learning:

1. Effective use of and monitoring the impact of homework and classwork

2. Use of amnesty days and periods

3. Use of MEAECs for missed, incomplete, or below mastery tasks

Effective Use of Homework as Practice

In Chapter 3, we discussed how traditions often overshadow evidence in grading practices, particularly regarding homework (see Figure 11.1). Homework is intended to help students practice, reinforce, and apply new skills while fostering independent learning. However, research suggests that less homework is more effective. For instance, Japan, which ranks second globally in education, assigns an average of only 3.8 hours of homework per week, compared to the United States, which ranks 17th with 6.1 hours (Teach.com, 2017, January 12).

The focus of homework should be on the quality of practice rather than the quantity; after all, practice doesn't make perfect, it makes permanent. Assuming that homework can yield the same learning outcomes without feedback and monitoring undermines the teacher's role (Nagel, 2015). Grading homework to enforce compliance—such as giving zeros for incomplete or late assignments—raises the question of whether low grades reflect a lack of learning or simply a lack of compliance (Vatterott, 2014).

Homework Mustn't Become a Losing Game

Goldberg (2007) spoke of the trap students find themselves caught in. They get behind in completing or submitting homework, which leads to lower grades or zeros that lower their overall grade (unrelated and likely inaccurate to their overall achievement). This causes a chain reaction by their teacher and parents, which leads to counter reactions by the student that can become cumulative. This creates experiences for students affecting their attitudes and performance for years. Incomplete homework → poor grades → poor attitudes → predictable avoidance of homework and a resentment toward the class, their teacher, or their school as a whole → More failing grades (Vatterott, 2014). This negative cycle negates any possible positive effects of homework and derails our ability to evaluate student progress. When the focus is on compliance of completion, not progress, even worse, it exacerbates the frustration students feel and endure. The more teachers and professional learning community (PLC teams) embrace and use the assessment/task grading matrix on a regular basis to evaluate the merits and benefits of any homework/classroom practice tasks, the more likely they are to avoid situations like Goldberg's trap.

FIGURE 11.1: ASSIGNMENT/TASK GRADING MATRIX

	Low Improvement of Learning and Achievement	High Improvement of Learning and Achievement
High Improvement of Grade	**Coasting** — Tasks lead to grade increases with no increase in learning or achievement	**Thriving** — Increase of learning and achievement along with increase in academic grade
Low Improvement of Grade	**Losing** — Grade either stays same or decreases with no increase in learning/achievement	**Developing** — Learning/achievement increases without an increase in academic grade

Elementary Considerations

Homework (d = 0.29), like many influences, has moderating effects and differences of impact for different students. Not surprisingly, the effects are highest for high school students and lowest for elementary. This has caused many elementary schools to abandon homework, which may not be in their best interest when parents judge the effectiveness of schools by the presence or amount of homework. The aim should be instead to improve the effect of homework (Hattie, 2023).

Figure 11.2 is a snapshot of some research to guide and impact decision-making related to homework. We developed a question to consider before reading each statement or summary. Please read through them, and reflect on how each statement and the question posed currently does or could impact you, your PLCs, or your schools grading actions.

FIGURE 11.2: EXAMPLES OF EFFECTIVE HOMEWORK RESEARCH AND CONSIDERATIONS

RESEARCH	CONSIDERATIONS FOR PRACTICE IN YOUR SCHOOL OR CLASSROOM

Does homework in your school or classroom promote a culture or practice or a culture of compliance?
 	
The nature of homework makes a difference: Homework that entails the deliberate practice of something already taught has a higher effect than requiring studying new or higher order ideas (Hattie, 2023).
 	
Trautwein et al. (2002) warned against homework that undermined a student's motivation and led to the student internalizing incorrect routines; instead, they found support for short frequent homework that the teachers closely monitored.
 	
1. In summary, Hattie's (2009, p. 235) synthesis on the effectiveness of homework on achievement found the following:
   a. Task-oriented homework had greater effects than deep learning problem solving.
   b. Rote learning and practice or rehearsal had the highest effects.
	• Includes purposeful practice
	• Provide frequent monitoring
	• Has task-oriented focus

RESEARCH	CONSIDERATIONS FOR PRACTICE IN YOUR SCHOOL OR CLASSROOM
Does the culture or practice of homework in our school convey too much reliance on parental involvement? There is negative impact on learning (−0.19) when there is too much parent surveillance of homework (Boonk et al., 2018; Clinton & Hattie, 2013). Homework should focus on opportunities to practice what has been taught deliberately and not require parental surveillance (Hattie, 2023). Parent support for autonomous student behavior showed a positive relationship to achievement whereas direct instructional involvement showed a negative relationship (Cooper, 2001).	Provide experiences that: - Involve minimal parent involvement - Include deliberate practice - Support student autonomy
Do we view homework as an extension of teaching and learning in the classroom *as needed for progress*? Children, as well as adults, have a limit to how much mental work they can accomplish in a day before the brain needs down time to process information (Jensen, 2000). Buell (2004) found that homework did work on one set of students but failed to work on another because of varying sets of expectations and experiences throughout the homework. Homework should be monitored more closely with an emphasis on progress with improvement noted and praised (Wright, 2006).	- Account for cognitive limits - Ensure consistent expectations - Close monitoring - Emphasize improvement

The following are some evidence-based, adaptable guidelines to consider related to using homework to support students driving their learning. Numbers are not in order or importance.

RECOMMENDATION	CONSIDERATIONS FOR ADAPTATION INTO MY CLASSROOM/PLCs PRACTICE
1. For younger students, encourage parents to partner in reinforcing skills and concepts at home, not just completing assignments.	• Develop parent workshops • Create clear guidelines • Promote collaborative learning • Offer regular feedback • Use homework diaries or journals • Encourage positive reinforcement • Establish clear communication channels • Provide sample activities
2. Provide success criteria. Target the experience of any homework as a means to practice essential concepts and skills *taught during that day's lesson.* Students not present in class that day need not be assigned to practice concepts that they were not present to learn.	• Define clear success criteria • Align homework with daily lessons • Adjust assignments for absences • Communicate expectations • Monitor and adjust homework • Provide support resources • Use formative assessments • Encourage reflection • Facilitate PLC discussions
3. Encourage and incentivize deliberate practice by rewarding students with less problems/ questions for demonstration of progress (e.g., ten problems assigned, students finishes when they get seven done correctly).	• Define clear progress indicators • Create a reward system • Communicate the system clearly • Monitor student progress • Incorporate formative assessments • Provide feedback • Foster a growth mindset • Collaborate in PLCs
4. Eliminate any busywork unrelated to learning goals to minimize compliance of completion.	• Align homework with learning objectives • Evaluate existing assignments • Gather student feedback • Incorporate authentic learning tasks • Prioritize quality over quantity • Differentiate assignments • Collaborate in PLCs • Communicate the purpose of assignments • Reflect and adjust

RECOMMENDATION	CONSIDERATIONS FOR ADAPTATION INTO MY CLASSROOM/PLCs PRACTICE

5. Encourage a balanced homework load:
   a. Manageable to not overwhelm students
   b. Collaborate across PLCs/course teams regarding homework expectations (See San Ramone Valley Policy)
	• Set clear guidelines
	• Coordinate across courses
	• Assess homework load
	• Focus on quality, not quantity
	• Incorporate flexible deadlines
	• Differentiated assignments
	• Provide homework support
	• Promote time-management skills
	• Regular check-ins
	• Encourage reflective practice
	• Communicate with parents

6. Ensure teacher feedback (marking, scoring for all homework):
   c. If it's important to assign, it must be important to check and monitor for learning not (just) completion.
   d. Provide constructive feedback, help students recognize mistakes to improve for learning not simply to add to grade
	• Establish clear feedback protocols
	• Timely feedback
	• Constructive and specific feedback
	• Use rubrics
	• Feedback sessions
	• Encourage self-assessment
	• Peer review
	• Monitor learning progress
	• Feedback for growth
	• Parental involvement
	• Professional development

7. Encouraging students to reflect on their homework experience can also foster self-regulation and independent learning skills (See four-box example in Chapter 12)	• Reflection prompts • Reflection journals • Post-homework discussions • Self-assessment checklists • Goal setting • Feedback incorporation • Teacher modeling • Parent involvement • Professional development • Student-led conferences

Example of Homework Policy Supporting Effective Practices

San Ramon Valley Unified School District in California has adopted some specific language to help support teacher practice. The following is an excerpt of the districtwide homework policy applicable to all grades:

- "Homework should be purposeful and meaningful to students. Legitimate purposes for homework include:
  - practicing a skill or process that students can do independently but not fluently,
  - elaborating on information that has been addressed in class to deepen students' knowledge, and providing opportunities for students to explore topics of their own interest.
- *Teachers are responsible for assigning homework that is appropriate and differentiated as needed."*

To view the San Ramone Valley Full Policy, scan the QR code here:

https://bit.ly/3Y8idi5

Amnesty Days

Amnesty days are designated and scheduled instructional periods devoted to supporting students who are struggling with skill development, concept mastery, or missing assignments, allowing them to catch up without penalties or grade reductions. Amnesty means obliterating the ramifications of an offense and comes from the same etymology as amnesia—we are forgetting about the penalty. Implementing amnesty days or periods periodically has multiple benefits for teachers and students:

1. Address some of the root causes of student failure and diminished progress in their learning
   a. Students missing multiple assignments
   b. Students getting too far behind in content understanding and feeling defeated and frustrated

2. Provide structured time for reteaching of critical skills for students

3. Promote student confidence in getting caught up in needed work completion but also in developing perseverance in doing so

Curriculum Benefits

Ainsworth (2011, p. 81) recommends buffers, or scheduled designated days or weeks for reteaching critical content during units of study. As mentioned, *amnesty days* benefit teachers as they provide opportunities for reteaching or reinforcing concepts and skills within the curriculum. We all know that, over the course of a 180-day school year, both teachers and students need a day or a few days to reteach or get caught up. This scheduled time also allows students who need it to get support from teachers that addresses specific gaps that led to the potential failure. The intentionality of scheduling it and conveying to students that a lifeline is coming allows students to see hope.

Origination of Concept of Amnesty Days

Dave's late colleague, Larry Hurt, a beloved art teacher at Ben Davis High School in Indianapolis (serving 2,900 students in Grades 10–12), introduced amnesty days to help struggling students catch up on missing assignments without penalty. Initially met with skepticism, the idea was implemented schoolwide and yielded positive results.

Following the first amnesty day, data revealed a 30 percent reduction in students at risk of failing, with attendance at an all-time high. Teachers noted that students who used this opportunity became more engaged and did not fall behind in subsequent weeks. Students reported increased confidence and improved grades.

Despite these successes, some teachers raised concerns about students potentially delaying work until the next amnesty day. To address this, adjustments were made: Amnesty days were unannounced, and each department or course team scheduled at least two per semester. This approach allowed teachers to plan strategically when to offer catch-up opportunities.

Overall, amnesty days proved successful at Ben Davis High School as being one of the actions that led to an increased graduation rate of 14 percent in four years (Nagel, 2008). By providing dedicated time for students to focus on missing work, both teachers and students observed improvements in academic performance and engagement, making it a valuable tool to combat failing grades due to incomplete assignments.

Nagel (2015)

A common question is, What about students who have completed all assignments during amnesty days? Typically, they can work on assignments or tasks from other classes or work on enrichment activities to boost their grade. Yet, most may simply enjoy the freedom that motivates adolescents. Behavioral expectations, such as punctuality and adherence to school rules, remain unchanged for all students, regardless of their need for amnesty support. Rarely are students who are all caught up with classwork ones that cause behavioral issues.

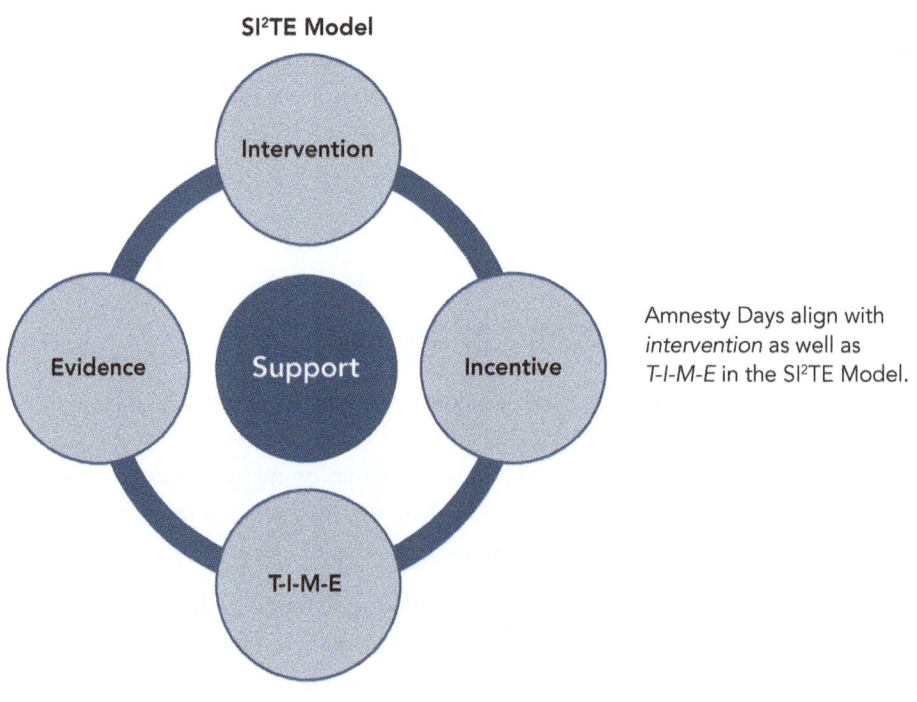

Amnesty Days align with *intervention* as well as *T-I-M-E* in the SI²TE Model.

MEAEC-it-Happen

Several authors and researchers have quipped that "The penalty for students not doing their work should be doing their work" (O'Connor, 2009, 2010; Reeves, 2011; Wormeli, 2006). We slightly disagree, we believe the penalty for students not doing assigned work should be doing the *right* work!

MEAEC stands for *Missing Essential Assignments or Assessments Extended Chance*. As we have alluded to, not all assignments or tasks are created equally in terms of rigor, challenge, complexity, demonstration of skill mastery, or even necessity (see assignment/task grading matrix). We also believe not every assignment or task is of equal importance to all students. MEAEC is a valuable practice that allows students to complete missed or poorly done assignments, focusing on aligning tasks for students with the essential skills *they need to improve upon*.

Teachers and teams provide (make-up) tasks to students that are essential and targeted to their learning needs. Teachers ensure *student tasks are related to specific areas the students need support in moving forward with curriculum goals*—not to simply complete missed work for the sake of completing missed work (Nagel, 2015). (See four-box examples in Chapter 12.)

Going Beyond ZAPs

Many schools implement ZAP (Zeros Aren't Permitted) programs to help students avoid falling too far behind in their grades due to missed assignments. While this is a commendable effort, it may inadvertently lead to superficial learning. If the focus is solely on having students complete work—regardless of quality or learning demonstrated—this approach undermines the value of genuine learning.

Students may receive the message that simply turning in tasks, even with minimal effort and without meaningful feedback, is sufficient to raise their grades. This discourages perseverance and persistence, as they learn that completion is valued over actual understanding. We have seen schools where students are required to attend study halls or after school sessions to finish assignments, and while this strategy aims to prevent failure, it *actually* promotes the *culture of completion compliance* rather than authentic learning, which does not at all foster the development of visible learners.

VIGNETTES

Back at Anywhere Middle School, students filled the library after classes, not for tutoring or extracurriculars, but to tackle a backlog of assignments from earlier in the year. The atmosphere was heavy with frustration, punctuated by sighs and rustling papers. These assignments, hastily prepared by teachers, lacked relevance to the current curriculum or student interests. They were mere busywork aimed at padding gradebooks and eliminating zeros that threatened averages.

Caden flipped through a thick math packet, his eyes glazing over at the repetitive problems. "Why do we even have to do this?" he mumbled to his friend Ava, equally engrossed in a history worksheet. "It's just to get a passing grade," she shrugged, highlighting passages in her textbook. "Mrs. Harper said it's to prevent failing, but I heard that as long as we submit them—even if they're wrong—we get full credit!"

Alex from Mrs. Rodriguez's science class overheard them, trying to grasp scientific concepts during the ZAP session to improve his grade. He shifted his focus from mastering material to simply completing assignments.

(Continued)

(Continued)

Around them, other students shared the same sense of futility, working mechanically checking boxes without thought. The joy of learning faded, as assignments became hoops to jump through instead of opportunities for growth. Burdened by administrative pressures, teachers viewed this as a necessary evil to keep students from slipping through the cracks. In this cycle, the joy of learning was overshadowed by the relentless quest to ensure passing grades. •

Maximizing Efforts to Support Struggling Students

The concept of MEAECs puts initiatives, like ZAPs, on steroids by ensuring students focus on assignments and tasks that align with student's individual learning needs. Approaches like this can be implemented schoolwide, within collaborative teams, or at individual teacher's levels. In all cases, it offers students a chance to do more than just make up work and avoid failing grades, *but even more importantly,* gain learning in essential concepts and skills to move forward (Nagel, 2015). Teachers and PLCs are also then combating the culture of *completion compliance* by MEAEC tasks, assignments, and so on. Through helping students effectively demonstrate progress of crucial concepts and skills, MEAECs help foster a sense of responsibility and accountability among students when completing tasks, perhaps in amnesty sessions, focused *on their needed next steps for progress toward essential skills*. Noticing progress in their learning promotes visible learner traits while minimizing *the compliance of completion in students* (see Figure 11.3). Also, the more students provide tangible evidence of learning through MEAECs, the more teachers become aware of where progress is or isn't being made toward mastery, which allows them to make authentic adjustments for where they need to go next instructionally.

FIGURE 11.3: EXAMPLE MEAEC—AMNESTY DAY

AUGUST	SEPTEMBER	OCTOBER	NOVEMBER
2 Missing Assignments or tasks	1 Missing Assignment or tasks	No Missing Assignments or Tasks	Amnesty Day 11-14
Is it logical for students to complete August work in mid-November?			

Applying the MEAEC concept helps teachers identify tasks that best support struggling learners, fostering collaboration within PLCs on grading and feedback. This approach results in more engaging and challenging assignments tailored to students' specific learning needs.

VIGNETTES

New School, New Approaches, New Alex!

After transferring to Wonder Middle School, Alex faced familiar academic challenges in eighth grade but found a supportive environment that transformed his experience. His science teacher, Mrs. Clark, greeted him with a smile and clearly outlined class objectives, emphasizing understanding over mere assignment completion. This approach contrasted sharply with his previous school, allowing Alex to see a roadmap for his learning.

When Alex and some classmates struggled with a complex unit on cellular biology, Mrs. Clark implemented an amnesty day before the unit's end, allowing students to catch up on essential work without penalty. She utilized the MEAEC concept, providing targeted assignments that aligned with their needs rather than just what was missing in her gradebook. "It's not just about deadlines," she said, "but mastering the material." This flexibility gave Alex the breathing room to grasp the topic at his own pace. See Appendix 15 for a sample Amnesty Day Menu.

Other teachers at Wonder Middle School, like Mr. Patel in math and Ms. Thompson in English, also prioritized understanding over busywork. They offered tutoring sessions and designed assignments that focused on comprehension and application. As a result, Alex engaged in after-school study groups and one-on-one sessions, where teachers patiently clarified difficult concepts until *he understood them*.

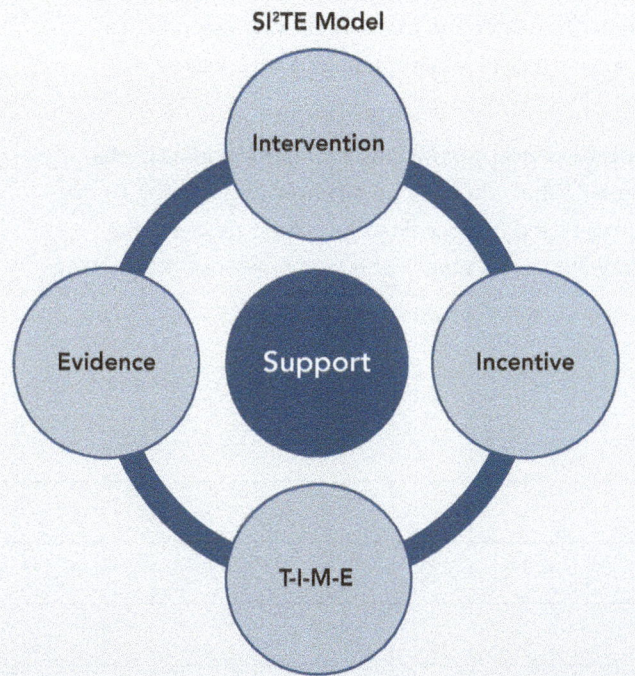

Study groups align with *support*, and having students focus on essential work with success aligns with *evidence* in the SI²TE Model.

(Continued)

(Continued)

Gradually, Alex's confidence rebuilt as he saw progress in his grades and became more comfortable asking questions. The teachers at Wonder Middle celebrated his small victories, reinforcing his belief in his abilities. "You're capable of understanding anything with the right support," Ms. Thompson often reminded him.

This transformation was significant. Alex re-engaged with his studies, eagerly participating in discussions and completing assignments with newfound purpose. The supportive practices at Wonder not only helped him understand concepts better but also restored his self-esteem and love for learning.

Alex's journey exemplifies how the right educational practices and nurturing environments enable students to overcome challenges and thrive academically. Now excited about entering high school, he said, "I know I'm not going to be a scientist, but the teachers gave me the chance to enjoy it and helped me keep up so much better."

 **CHAPTER REFLECTION**

1. How could you plan for amnesty days (periods) to promote student learning and desired learner behaviors?

2. What are some ways you might better and more effectively use practice and classroom/homework to promote student learning and desired learner behaviors?

3. How could you implement the concept of MEAECs to help students better determine learning progress? What would be an example of gathering better evidence of student learning based on specific tasks related to where the student needs to move forward versus simply what was previously assigned?

NOTES

_____

_____

_____

_____

_____

CHAPTER 12

Great Learners Are Successful in Recognizing Their Learning and Teach Others

"It's the teacher that makes the difference, not the classroom."

—Michael Morpurgo

The final piece in developing students who drive their learning is helping them recognize *their* learning and teach others. This trait is a culmination of the other five and begins with awareness of what and how they are learning. Once students achieve this awareness, they can become teachers of themselves and others. John Hattie emphasizes that true visible learning occurs when students teach and teachers learn.

In the movie *The Karate Kid*, the protagonist, Daniel LaRusso is a teenager from New Jersey who moves to California with his mom and seeks karate lessons from an elderly man, Mr. Miyagi to combat bullies. Miyagi agrees but trains him through having Daniel complete unusual chores around his house requiring him to use precise movements as he does. Initially eager, Daniel soon grows frustrated, feeling his tasks have nothing to do with karate and just jobs Miyagi doesn't want to do himself. He threatens to quit, but Miyagi demonstrates the connection by asking Daniel to showcase his newfound techniques. In a powerful scene, Daniel uses the movements from sanding floors, painting fences, and so on to successfully block Miyagi's strikes, realizing these chores taught him essential karate skills. This revelation rekindles his motivation to learn even more from Miyagi.

SUCCESS CRITERIA

As a reader, after reading this chapter, I will be able to

1. Determine strategies to intentionally support students in reflecting on their current learning results

2. Use rubrics to support students in becoming effective peer tutors

3. Identify success criteria to teach students how to correctly self and peer assess work

4. Implement a system for students and the teacher to monitor and provide feedback to collaborative work •

COMMONLY HELD BELIEFS	COUNTERPOINT
Giving students more work when they complete required work provides needed challenges and accelerates their learning.	Teachers' desire to push students to achieve more and accelerate their learning is well warranted. We error when we blanketly assume that students *should always* accept additional work/rigorous challenges simply because they have met learning targets *ahead of schedule or ahead of their peers.*
When students work collaboratively, teachers need to still grade them on their individual contribution and individual mastery of content.	Grading students individually in a collaborative setting often undermines the value of teamwork and minimizes the opportunity for students to focus on developing skills related to working together and developing collaborative speaking and listening skills. When teachers focus as much on individual performance when students are working in collaborative settings, students become less concerned about collective success and more with personal achievement. This prevents students from recognizing the benefits of sharing knowledge and teaching and learning from each other.

Visible Learner Trait and Adult Mindframe Focus for Chapter 12

- **G**auge their current level of understanding.
- **R**eadiness to know where they are going and are confident to take on the challenge.
- **A**dapt tools to guide their learning.
- **D**etermine feedback and recognize that errors are opportunities to learn.
- **E**valuate their progress and adjust their learning.
- Be **S**uccessful in recognizing their learning and teach others.

VISIBLE LEARNERS ARE SUCCESSFUL IN RECOGNIZING THEIR LEARNING AND TEACH OTHERS

Teaching others deepens our understanding, as many educators have experienced during moments of realization in their careers. How many times have we been teaching students and said to ourselves, *"OH...I JUST figured it out!"* John Hattie states that visible learning occurs when students teach and teachers learn, making this final trait a culmination of the previous five.

To promote this trait, we must focus on two key elements. First, students need opportunities for consistent reflection on their learning to be successful in recognizing it. They must engage in the assessment process to fully understand both their successes and struggles.

Second, we must empower students to be both their own teachers and teachers of others. Collaborative learning and peer tutoring are effective strategies that facilitate this transfer of knowledge. As Seneca said, "While we teach, we learn." Establishing a culture of collaboration enables

(Continued)

> (Continued)
>
> students to share their thought processes, connections, and ideas, reinforcing their learning.
>
> By cultivating a classroom environment where collaboration and teaching are the norms, we foster visible learners who are engaged and empowered in their educational journey. •

Mindframes drive actions to support the development of students who are successful in recognizing their learning and teach others.

> 1. I engage as much in dialogue as monologue.
> 2. I focus on learning and the language of learning

Visible learners aren't born; they develop through effective classroom practices. Research shows that teachers have the most significant influence on student learning, second only to the students themselves. For students to recognize and share their learning, consistent interaction around what they are learning with peers is critical.

In classrooms where the teacher is viewed as the sole knowledge source, students struggle to share knowledge with peers. However, when teachers foster a language of learning that encourages student dialogue equal to teacher talk, students begin to see themselves as their own teachers and regard their classmates as valuable resources for learning.

Supporting Students to Respond to Current Results

Adult actions in schools are crucial for helping students transition from viewing learning as final to seeing it as fluid. Empowering students to take ownership of their learning and move away from mere *completion compliance* requires intentional reflection on their current progress.

Grading practices often hinder this shift by emphasizing completion and correctness rather than growth. Supporting students in evaluating their results is essential for making necessary adjustments. Nicol and Macfarlane-Dick (2006) argue that traditional feedback, often provided by teachers, deprives students of opportunities to become self-regulated learners capable of identifying their own errors. Therefore, it's vital to balance helping students recognize their achievements with guiding them in addressing their mistakes.

Let's consider the following two scenarios and revisit the *assignment grading matrix:*

SCENARIO ONE	SCENARIO TWO
At Anywhere Middle School, Mr. Pappas returns a recent social studies test with around forty items, showing students their grades based solely on the percentage of correct answers. He offers class time for students to use their books and notes to correct mistakes and submit them for half credit, which raises their grades. Most students quickly look up answers, revise their errors, and hand them in for points, showing minimal processing or connection-making in their learning. Their primary focus is merely completing the task to boost their grades.	At Wonder Middle School, Miss Hatcher teaches English/Language Arts and recently administered a test to her students. When returning tests or quizzes, she has students engage in a reflection activity to review both correct and incorrect answers. Students first identify the correct answers, then ask whether they were easy or challenging. Next, they analyze their missed questions by determining if they genuinely misunderstood the concepts and need reteaching. For others, they reflect on whether they made careless mistakes or require additional practice and feedback related to the assessed skills. She refers to this process as her Four-Box Reflection. (See Figure 12.1.)

FIGURE 12.1: FOUR-BOX REFLECTION TOOL

Difficult Questions/Tasks I **Got Correct**/Was *successful* with: _____ _____ _____ _____	Difficult Questions/Tasks I **Got Incorrect**/Was not *successful* with (Where I need help): _____ _____ _____ _____
Easy Questions/Tasks I **Got Correct** Was *successful* with: _____ _____ _____ _____	Easy Questions/Tasks I **Got Incorrect**/Was not *successful* with (Where I need to concentrate more or practice with feedback). _____ _____ _____ _____

SOURCE: Adapted from Fisher et al. (2024).

The four-box reflection (see Figure 12.1) tool will benefit both Miss Hatcher and her students. For her, it provides valuable information as to the level of challenge she provided her students. If many questions fall into the green (easy) box, the assessment may not be challenging enough. Conversely, if a disproportionate number of items are in the blue (difficult) box, she will need to invest time in reteaching certain concepts and skills. Finally, and most importantly for her and her students, is what items or questions are placed in the red box (lower right). These are questions or tasks that students have determined they made errors but understand why and where to go next. They either need to concentrate and focus more on the topic or concepts the questions were related to, or perhaps what is needed is time and practice with feedback.

WHAT I DID WELL (SPECIFIC QUESTIONS OR CRITERIA) GREEN OR YELLOW QUADRANTS	WHAT I NEED MY TEACHER TO HELP WITH OR RETEACH ME (SPECIFIC QUESTIONS OR CRITERIA) LIGHT BLUE QUADRANT	WHAT I NEED TO PRACTICE AND RECEIVE FEEDBACK ON (SPECIFIC QUESTIONS OR CRITERIA) RED QUADRANT

Actions I need to Take to Move Forward in My Learning:

How teachers would incorporate a tool like this when determining grades on a task, assessment, or test would of course vary. The key point is that providing learners with a reflection tool encourages them to focus less on simply fixing errors for grades and more on evaluating their learning progress and necessary adjustments. This absolutely fosters a view of learning with fluidity rather than finality.

REFLECT AND CONSIDER

How could you incorporate the four-box reflection to support students recognizing where they are in their learning? •

_____
_____
_____
_____

Peer Tutoring

Once students develop the ability to recognize when and how they're learning, they become empowered to begin to teach themselves and others. Students can now truly become drivers of their learning while being able to help move the learning of their peers as well. Peer tutoring does not simply mean students seated at the same table and working together or being assigned to *help* other students who are less proficient in understanding certain concepts or specific skills. Teachers sometimes claim to use peer tutoring to boost collaborative learning, but assigning students to work together without guidance and support will not be effective in increasing their learning (Topping, 2008). Structuring peer tutoring with guidance is essential for its success.

VIGNETTES

Back at Wonder Middle School

Ms. Johnson: I've been considering ways to make our science tasks more engaging. One improvement could be enhancing how we incorporate feedback, encouraging students to seek it actively and use it to advance their learning.

Mr. Patel: Great point, Ms. J. Feedback is essential for fostering a culture of thinking. I've implemented a feedback loop where students submit their experiment findings, receive detailed comments on their process, and then revise their work accordingly.

(Continued)

(Continued)

Ms. Garcia: That sounds really neat and would be super effective, Mr. Patel. I encourage my students to give and receive peer feedback. After presenting their project findings, classmates ask questions and offer suggestions, helping them refine their ideas and fostering critical thinking through evaluating each other's work.

Ms. Johnson: I love the idea of focusing the kids on peer feedback. This *totally* fosters a collaborative learning environment. I've actually just started to introduce reflection journals for my students to document their learning processes, challenges, and how they are using feedback to improve their work.

Mr. Patel: Reflection journals are fantastic. They encourage students to think about their thinking, which is so important. How do you assess them, Ms. Johnson?

Ms. Johnson: I use a rubric that emphasizes the clarity of reflections, response to feedback, and improvements made, focusing on growth over time. Creating a safe environment is crucial for students to share their struggles and successes.

Ms. Garcia: That's key—making sure they feel safe to take risks and make mistakes. I also like to have one-on-one feedback sessions with my students where we discuss their progress, feedback they received, and set goals for their next steps. It's a more personalized approach and helps them see the value of feedback in their learning process.

Mr. Patel: One-on-one sessions are always effective. I've noticed that when kids find the feedback meaningful they instantly have motivation to improve. For instance, in a recent project designing simple machines, my feedback on initial designs led to significant adjustments where some kids were bouncing ideas off of each other and totally led to much better final products.

Ms. Johnson: Feedback can indeed transform the learning process. I think we should also focus on teaching students how to seek feedback. They need to learn to ask specific questions like, "How can I make this part clearer?" or "What evidence can I add to strengthen my argument?"

Ms. Garcia: Yes, teaching them to seek feedback is crucial. I've started modeling this behavior by showing them how I would revise a piece of work based on feedback. They see that even their teacher is constantly improving, and it sets a positive example.

Ms. Johnson: As an agenda item for our next meeting, we will collaboratively design Universal Success Criteria for Using Feedback to Improve Scientific Inquiry as well as design a variety of tasks that will apply. This will focus our work on promoting critical thinkers.

Using the Clarity of Scoring Grading Matrix Figure 12.2, the team created a variety of examples to help generate experiences supporting students giving feedback. ●

FIGURE 12.2: CLARITY OF GRADING SCORING GUIDE (CGSG)

Mindframes for Learning: Which Is a Focus for This Unit/Lesson I engage as much in dialogue as monologue. I focus on learning and the language of learning	*Visible Learner Trait* Successful in recognizing their learning and teach others	
GENERATIVE LEARNING EXPERIENCES		**WEIGHTED SCORING**
SURFACE	**Scientific Inquiry Task:** "Exploring the Water Cycle Through Recall and Retrieval Practice" **Objective:** To help students understand and explain the water cycle by using recall and retrieval practice, making their thinking visible through diagrams and written explanations. **Seeking Feedback:** Students can proactively seek comprehensive feedback with detailed, thoughtful questions.	0.5X
	Scientific Inquiry Task: "Understanding and Processing Information About Photosynthesis" **Objective:** To help students understand and process information about photosynthesis through reading, discussing, and creating a conceptual model. **Using Feedback:** Students can make significant, effective changes in their work based on detailed feedback, showing clear improvement.	X
PRECIPICE OF COGNITIVE CHALLENGE		
DEEP	**Scientific Inquiry Task:** "Analyzing and Applying Concepts of Ecosystems and Food Webs" **Objective:** To help students apply, analyze, and link information about ecosystems and food webs by researching, constructing food webs, and evaluating the impact of changes within ecosystems. **Reflection on Feedback:** Students can deeply reflect on the feedback received, demonstrating significant insight and learning.	1.5X
TRANSFER	**Scientific Inquiry Task:** "Debating Renewable vs. Nonrenewable Energy Sources" **Objective:** To engage students in comparing renewable and nonrenewable energy sources, constructing arguments, and defending their positions through a structured debate. **Scaffold Feedback:** Students can offer examples of effective and useful feedback questions and model how to use feedback effectively.	2X

Peer and Self Grading

In *The Hidden Lives of Learners* (2007), Nuthall identified the 80-20 principle, noting that 80 percent of student feedback comes from peers, and 20 percent of that feedback is inaccurate. While this may suggest limiting peer feedback, it highlights the need for students to have clear success criteria guiding their evaluations.

Incorporating peer evaluations of work and performances allows students to both give and receive valuable feedback throughout the learning process. For instance, using simple rubrics enables students to self-evaluate their strengths and areas for improvement. Subsequently, during the next class, they can evaluate each other's work based on the same criteria. This process shifts students' perceptions of their learning and exposes them to diverse perspectives (Nicol & Macfarlane-Dick, 2006). After receiving peer feedback, students can reevaluate their work and make necessary adjustments, enhancing their metacognitive skills and fostering self-correction.

Success Criteria Up-Front

Transparent success criteria are most effective when given at the start of a task and understood by students. Conversely, if they are distributed just before administration of an assessment they prove to be very ineffective. Evidence shows that students' self-assessment and peer evaluation grades closely align with the teacher's evaluation, which would demonstrate that students were able to have a clear grasp of the success criteria. (Fisher et al., 2024).

Five Benefits and Considerations for Peer and Self Grading

1. <u>Not Just for the Bright Students</u>: Peer feedback is influential and should be integrated into the learning process to benefit all students, not just those perceived as stronger (Sadler & Good, 2006). We learn the most when teaching or at least attempting to impart our knowledge and understanding to others. Far too often there is a perception that certain strategies and actions are for certain students.

   While children vary dramatically in what they know, they still share the same learning algorithms. Thus the same pedagogical tricks that work best with all children are also those that tend to be most efficient for children with learning disabilities—they must be applied with only greater focus, patience, systematricity, and tolerance to error. (Dehaene, 2018)

2. <u>Minimizes Instruction and Grading as Separate Entities</u>: Teachers often see grading as a separate entity from teaching and learning, with feedback traditionally flowing only from teacher to student. This limits students' chances to become self-regulated learners capable of identifying their own errors. Nicol and Macfarlane-Dick (2006) argue for a more collaborative approach between teachers and students regarding classroom feedback and grading.

3. <u>Increases Students' Engagement and Reception to Feedback:</u> Peer and self-grading, enhances the impact of peer tutoring by increasing student talk. The more students are collaborating with each other and the more their level of engagement is increased, thus they are more likely to respond positively to feedback, even if it is corrective (Topping, 2020).

   Peer review and grading procedures can serve as the foundation for interactive classroom activities, driven by the teacher with success criteria as the catalyst.

4. <u>Saves Time</u>: Another benefit of peer and self grading is to the classroom teacher. These experiences can be quick and not time consuming. They then have the potential to provide feedback that is meaningful and integrated into the learning process without as much heavy lifting on the part of the teacher (Freeman & Parks, 2010). Integrating peer self-assessment and grading in the curriculum boosts student engagement, offers meaningful feedback, promotes equity and accessibility, and reduces the time teachers spend providing detailed feedback on assignments.

5. <u>Blend in Anonymous Peer-Grading</u>: Time is needed to create the culture for students to be able to, even with criteria, be effective and accurate in their feedback and peer-grading. Sadler and Good (2006) examined self-grading and peer grading in middle-school classrooms. They found that when the identity of the learner was blinded initially, so as not to socially influence the peer grader, the students learned how to be more accurate before moving into working with specific peers with their own work. Most importantly, students learned how to evaluate their work using the criteria outlined in the rubrics, which is the key takeaway.

STUDENT	INITIAL SELF GRADE AGAINST CRITERIA	PEER GRADE	PEER FEEDBACK	FINAL SELF GRADE AGAINST CRITERIA	TEACHER SPOT CHECK ON FINAL GRADES AGAINST CRITERIA
Steve	B−	C	Specific by student	B+	B+
Aiden J.	C	C+	Specific by student	B+	A−
DK	A	B	Specific by student	B+	A−
Holly	D	C	Specific by student	B−	
Maria	B	C	Specific by student	B+	
Aiden H.	C	C+	Specific by student	B	B
Jacob	C	C−	Specific by student	B+	

Teacher did not go back and check every student final grade against criteria

COMMENTS FROM STUDENTS WHOSE TEACHERS UTILIZE PEER AND SELF-GRADING
Sam (Fourth Grade): "Once I get the feedback and grade from my peers I get excited because I know I can take that and get a better grade."
Amelia (Twelfth Grade): "I love giving feedback and a draft grade to my peers. That alone helps me instantly see more clearly what I need to do when revising my work."
Doug (Ninth Grade): "It wasn't easy providing my peers grades the first few times. I was worried that if I gave them a low (even if it was honest) grade, they might get mad. Mrs. Jones has helped us all realize the more we are honest in what we see in each other's work related to the criteria, the more we will learn and the more our grades will get better over the semester."
Stephanie (Second Grade): "I really look forward to peer editing and grading time in reading and math. It's so much fun to hear how my classmates think of my work and if their thinking is like mine. It's fun to fix it and make it better before we turn it in with our recommended grade."
Billy Ray (Seventh Grade): "At first I didn't like it (peer and self grading), it seemed like extra work. I was so used to just getting my work done and turning it in hoping I'd get enough points. Now, I know that my job is to not only make my work better and strive for the higher grade I deserve (because it's against the criteria), but my job is to help my friends get a better grade, too, by showing them what's missing or needs work on their assignments."

REFLECT AND CONSIDER

How do you/does your PLC team support developing your students' ability to effectively engage in collaboration related to peer and self grading?

_____
_____
_____
_____
_____

Grading Behaviors of Visible Learners—Collaboration

In Chapter 2, we made the case that our job as teachers of third grade, middle school social studies, biology, or so on is never first to develop great students of third grade, middle school social studies, biology but rather to develop great learners and those that are in the driver's seat of that learning. Recognizing learning to then teach others requires students to collaborate with each other.

Virtually every job or trade our students will acquire when they enter into the workforce will require some degree of effective collaboration. Teachers and PLC teams must weave teaching collaboration into the instruction of their curriculum while helping students recognize how they use collaboration to teach themselves and others.

CORE PRACTICE

Joe Smith and his ninth-grade PLC at *Wonder High School* reconvened for a team meeting prior to starting the second semester. They have been working very hard as a team to help students develop assessment capabilities and become better and stronger learners. They know that their classroom actions and approaches are directly tied and related to the behaviors they often see develop in their students. One area that they felt their students struggled in the first semester was related to effective collaboration and classroom discussions with peers. As recent middle school students, some of this was likened to a lack of maturity. The team knew this was also related to teachers not being intentional in teaching students *how to have an effective discussion* and providing students clarity on how to determine what effective collaboration would look like.

The team believed by providing students with clear criteria for student collaborative activities, they would see more of the behaviors they hoped to cultivate displayed by students. The team turned to the Common Core speaking and listening standards as a guide and focused on four (see Figure 12.3). See Appendix 16, Sample Group Roles.

The Common Core speaking and listening standards provide teachers with concrete targets to assess students and give feedback on essential collaboration skills. These are essential for students to develop to become college and career ready. The Common Core spiraling provides clear learning progressions for teachers to use for feedback, student self-assessment and growth, and potential criterion-based grading targets.

CCSSI states,

> To become college and career ready, students must have ample opportunities to participate in various rich, structured conversations—as part of a whole class, in small groups, and with a partner—built around important content in various domains. Whatever their intended major or profession,

(Continued)

(Continued)

high school graduates will depend heavily on their ability to listen attentively to others so that they are able to build on others' meritorious ideas while expressing their own clearly and persuasively. (Nagel, 2015, p. 48)

FIGURE 12.3: COMMON CORE STATE STANDARDS

SL9-10.1a	**Come to discussions prepared, having read and researched material under study;** explicitly draw on that preparation by **referring to evidence from texts and other research on the topic** or issue to stimulate a thoughtful, well-reasoned exchange of ideas.
SL9-10.1b	**Work with peers to set rules for collegial discussions and decision-making** (e.g., informal consensus, taking votes on key issues, presentation of alternate views), **clear goals and deadlines, and individual roles as needed.**
SL9-10.1C	**Propel conversations by posing and responding to questions that relate the current discussion to broader themes** or larger ideas; **actively incorporate others into the discussion;** and clarify, verify, or challenge ideas and conclusions.
SL9-10.1d	**Respond thoughtfully to diverse perspectives, summarize points of agreement and disagreement,** and, when warranted, qualify or justify their own views and understanding and **make new connections in light of the evidence and reasoning presented.**

SOURCE: Reprinted from Nagel (2015).

The team also felt it was important to empower students to self-evaluate their collaborative efforts. Teachers let students score (grade) themselves related to these targets as well as set short-term goals for what they need to improve on. Similar to the previous peer grading example, teachers spot checked certain students' scores. What they found more often than not was the need to coach the student to a *higher* grade where the student scored themselves lower than the teacher felt they would have (see Figure 12.4).

When the team met several weeks into the second semester, they were extremely pleased at the growth in their students' ability to engage in classroom discussions and determine their specific next steps. One student quipped, *"I feel so much stronger in my ability to know how to engage with my classmates in debates about what we are learning. I am able to be so much better at gathering my thoughts during discussions and reflect on what my classmates share as well."*

(100 Points Possible) •

FIGURE 12.4: COLLABORATIVE GRADING RUBRIC

		GRADING RUBRIC (100 POINTS)		
	Student-friendly success criteria (Students check ones met; teacher has veto rights)	I haven't been consistent in applying these strategies or haven't made sufficient effort to do so (0 points—checked off 3 or fewer) Practice/second-chance sessions on second Thursday of the month for second-chance time with teacher	I am continually demonstrating improvement on using and applying these strategies through practice and receiving feedback (15 points for 4 or 5 out of 7)	I regularly and successfully use these strategies (18 points for 6 or 7)
SL9-10.1a **Come to discussions prepared, having read and researched material under study**; explicitly draw on that preparation by **referring to evidence from texts and other research on the topic** or issue to stimulate a thoughtful, well-reasoned exchange of ideas.	I prepare for class or team discussions, having read and researched material assigned to the group or class.			
	I explicitly refer to evidence from texts to make sure the discussion is rich and thoughtful.			
SL.9-10.1b **Work with peers to set rules for collegial discussions and decision-making** (e.g., informal consensus, taking votes on key issues, presentation of alternate views), **clear goals and deadlines, and individual roles as needed.**	I help my peers create rules for discussion, and ensure that I adhere to them.			
	When necessary, I support the group discussion by addressing norm violations that get in the way of group learning.			

(Continued)

(Continued)

Standard	Self-Description			
SL.9-10.1c **Propel conversations by posing and responding to questions that relate the current discussion to broader themes** or larger ideas; **actively incorporate others Into the discussion**; and clarify, verify, or challenge ideas and conclusions.	I help move the discussion forward by making sure my responses to the questions relate to the topic and bigger picture in a mature and focused approach.			
SL9-10.1d **Respond thoughtfully to diverse perspectives, summarize points of agreement and disagreement**, and, when warranted, qualify or justify their own views and understanding and **make new connections In light of the evidence and reasoning presented.**	I comment back to peers by first summarizing their points (where we agree or disagree).			
	My point allotment for this 2-week cycle: _____/100 My Improvement Goal for the next 2 weeks is _____. I will specifically focus on _____ and seek help, coaching, and assistance from (my teacher) _____ and (peers) _____ and _____.			

SOURCE: Nagel (2015).

REFLECT AND CONSIDER

How could providing success criteria for desired collaborative behaviors increase the quality and impact of classroom discussion in your school or classroom?

_____
_____
_____
_____
_____

CHAPTER REFLECTION

1. How will you intentionally support students in reflecting on their current learning results?
2. What are some ways you can use rubrics to support students in becoming effective peer tutors?
3. How could you implement processes for self and peer assessment of individual and collaborative work?

NOTES

_____
_____
_____
_____
_____
_____
_____

NOTES

CHAPTER 13

Effective Grading Is a Critical Component of the Practice of Teaching

"In ninth grade, I came up with a new form of rebellion. I hadn't been getting good grades, but I decided to get all A's without taking a book home. I didn't go to math class, because I knew enough and had read ahead, and I placed within the top 10 people in the nation on an aptitude exam."

—Bill Gates

Teachers work exceptionally hard to teach and develop their students both academically and to develop behaviors that enhance their learning. Grading is by far the one element that can bolster or undergird or derail or stonewall everything else we do in our schools and classrooms. The struggle for effective grading could be equivalent to (more) than a 100 year war (Starch & Elliott, 1912). Despite knowing so much more in 2025 than we ever have before about what best impacts student learning, grading traditions far too often still trump evidence of effective practice.

We have attempted to provide evidence-based and practical, yet adaptable, strategies and concepts for teachers and school leaders to use when tackling this challenge. Our model for improving grading actions is not an all-inclusive list actions nor a specific recipe that must be followed precisely. Every school and classroom may look different in their implementation and use of the strategies and concepts we have outlined. They do provide specific focused actions and approaches to tackle some of the challenges related to grading and move well past philosophical conversations that never lead to classroom practice. Most importantly they help shift the narrative of viewing learning with *fluidity not finality!*

SUCCESS CRITERIA

As a reader, after reading this chapter, I will be able to

1. Determine strategies to intentionally support students developing the traits of a visible learner through my grading practices
2. Apply the mindframes for learning in my approach to my grading practices
3. Implement core grading practices within my professional learning community (PLC)

Develop Great Learners, Not Good Students

Students who take charge of their learning exhibit specific traits essential for academic success and personal growth. All educator actions need to be aligned to promoting these within our students. These traits, nurtured by effective teaching practices and grading strategies, include the following:

1. **Gauge Current Level of Understanding:** Learners need to know their starting point and destination. Teachers must clearly communicate learning goals and how students will demonstrate them. Tasks and assignments should provide evidence and feedback for both students and teachers to determine the next steps in learning.

2. **Readiness for Challenges:** Tasks should be appropriately challenging—neither too difficult nor too easy. Tasks that don't allow students to apply skills beyond basic understanding are seen as busywork. Such tasks should be meaningful, encouraging students to consider what learning is needed and what comes next.

3. **Adapt Tools for Learning:** Avoid early grading. Early grades can shift focus from learning strategies to grades. Harsh early grades can discourage students from moving forward, while high early grades can lead to overconfidence or the fear of taking risks. Both scenarios deter students from taking on new challenges and risks.

4. **Recognize Feedback as Opportunities:** Foster a classroom culture that views errors as learning opportunities. Penalize careless errors appropriately, linking penalties to the effort required to correct them. Ensure that the environment supports learning from mistakes.

5. **Evaluate and Adjust Learning:** Encourage self-regulation by allowing students to determine which strategies work best for them. Promote ownership of learning by providing multiple paths and options, avoiding a one-size-fits-all approach.

6. **Be Successful in Recognizing Their Learning and Teach Others:** Encourage peer learning. Students often learn best when teaching others. Ensure students understand success criteria to provide accurate feedback to peers. Facilitate focused collaboration, enabling students to teach and learn from each other effectively.

Apply the Mindframes for Learning

When teachers view themselves as evaluators of their impact and believe in every student's potential, they foster a supportive environment that motivates students. This belief allows teachers to create tasks that provide valuable evidence for enhancing students' self-awareness regarding their progress. By consistently assessing and giving constructive feedback, teachers help students identify strengths and areas for improvement. This process encourages reflection, helping students understand their comprehension levels and to set achievable goals, promoting ownership of their academic growth. While Hattie emphasizes nine mindframes for effective teaching, the primary focus must be on evaluating our impact on student learning. Embracing this mindset equips teachers to identify and replicate effective practices, including grading, while avoiding less effective approaches.

Implement Core Grading Actions

Effective grading practices are critical in supporting student-driven learning and reinforcing the traits of visible learners. The following actions, grounded in research and evidence, are essential:

- **Teacher Collaboration:**
  - Collaborative PLC teams focus ongoing dialogue on grading actions. Example topics include assignment analysis, agreement on success criteria expected for mastery, failure prevention strategies, accurate weighing of student work evidence toward grade, and so on.

- **Clarity of Scoring:**
  - Teachers determine how student work and product evidence are produced and aligned to success criteria and rigor of task(s). These are communicated to students to support their understanding of how to interpret feedback through grades.

> The catalyst of effectiveness in instruction, assessment, and feedback is teacher clarity. We must include clarity of scoring as a nonnegotiable element as well.
>
> *We have developed and shared numerous examples of the Clarity of Grading Scoring Guide to assist teachers and teams when planning and developing, assignments, assessments, tasks, performance, and so on. When we look to provide feedback to students in the form of a grade we must acknowledge the differences in rigor and complexity of cognitive demand. Thus, those that do, must have a great weight related to a student's overall grade.* •

- **Collaborative Scoring and Collaborative Feedback:**
  - Teachers work together to score and grade student work and products with common understanding of criteria. Teachers also share and discuss what feedback would be most impactful to move students' learning forward.
- **Multiple Opportunities for Success and Mastery Through the Use of Stipulated Second Chances:**
  - Teachers and collaborative teams provide students with multiple opportunities for success and to progress toward mastery. These come with *stipulations*, such as additional work or time commitments for students to develop habits conducive to being good learners but not a reduction in points or marks to devalue their overall grade.

Utilize the SI²TE Model

The SI²TE model provides a structured approach to support students through their learning challenges. Its implementation involves the following:

1. **Support:**
   - Students feel support from their teachers in taking risks in their learning. This leads to confidence they can overcome challenges they face in their learning journey.
2. **Intervention:**
   - Teachers and collaborative teams do not wait when they notice student(s) struggling in their learning. Systems are in place both at the school and classroom levels to be decisive in instructional moves and approaches to intervene and adjust to student learning needs.

3. **Incentives:**
   - Teachers develop systems of actions to incentivize students toward achievement and desired behaviors versus a system of consequences. This is different from rewards in that adult actions focus on deepening student motivation for a fuller understanding of topics and content.

4. **Time:**
   - Teachers and collaborative teams always view time as the variable and learning as the constant. Progress and growth are always primary drivers versus just focusing on achievement.

5. **Evidence:**
   - Teachers and collaborative teams are relentless in their pursuit of supporting students in their next steps of learning. This requires making adjustments in assessment strategies and tools to ensure the best and most accurate evidence of student learning is the focus of student work and performance expectations.

View Teaching as a Practice

Doctors practice medicine, attorneys practice law, and thus educators practice teaching. We must embrace our profession as such and use actions that are proven to increase the probability of impacting learning and eliminate actions that have shown to diminish impact. We revisit Wonder School District one last time to review this practice in action.

VIGNETTES

At Wonder School District, leadership has transformed grading and feedback through the implementation of PLCs aimed at enhancing classroom cohesion (d = 0.66). Classroom cohesion is characterized by the collaborative effort of teachers and students working together toward positive learning goals, fostering an equitable and respectful environment that supports all students on their learning journeys.

Each week, teachers from different grade levels and subjects convene in their PLCs to discuss and refine grading practices. They believe that assessment should serve as a learning tool rather than a conclusive judgment. This collaboration promotes clear, fair, and supportive grading methods, reinforcing the idea that teachers and students are partners in education.

(Continued)

(Continued)

A vital aspect of this initiative is clarity in scoring. Teachers collaboratively develop detailed rubrics that outline expectations for each assignment, sharing these with students at the beginning to clarify what is required for each grade level. This transparency empowers students to take ownership of their learning, enabling them to self-assess their progress and identify areas for improvement.

Another cornerstone of Wonder School District's approach is collaborative grading with feedback that guides students on their next learning steps. During PLC meetings, teachers grade samples of students' work together, ensuring consistency and fairness in grading while sharing insights and strategies. This exchange fosters a deeper understanding of effective teaching methods to support student learning.

Feedback is regarded as essential to the learning process, with errors seen not as failures but as growth opportunities. Students are encouraged to revise and improve their work based on constructive feedback focused on specific improvement areas. This iterative process helps cultivate resilience and a growth mindset, ensuring that grading supports ongoing learning rather than being final.

Overall, Wonder School District's effective grading practices enhance self-efficacy for both students and teachers. By promoting collaboration, clarity, and continuous improvement, the district helps everyone see their potential. This focus on equitable, respectful learning ensures that every student can succeed and grow, fostering a supportive and cohesive classroom community. ●

Conclusion

Like most important endeavors in life, effective grading requires investment—in time, effort, and thoughtful reflection. Effective grading involves careful thought and actions that require a pathway to fair, transparent, and growth-oriented feedback. This journey requires ongoing reflection and adaptation. We thank you for allowing us to offer some guidance to become an even more effective educator, dedicated to your students' success and growth.

Dave and Bruce

REFLECT AND CONSIDER:

How will you deliberately practice teaching through grading visible learners?

NOTES

NOTES

Afterword

The Exciting Future for Grading Visible Learners

by John Hattie, Emeritus Laureate Professor,
University of Melbourne, Australia

I have dedicated my academic life to investigating measurement, starting with the core question, "Is this test measuring but one thing (is this test unidimensional)?" Imagine a twenty-item test with ten spelling and ten math items. Any score would be meaningless as you do not know whether, for example, a score of 12 out of 20 included ten spelling items correct +2 math, or 10 math items +2 spelling. We can develop multidimensional tests and then meaningfully ask about the attributes of these multiple dimensions. I can wax lyrical about one-, two-, or three-parameter item test models, optimal test design, and even more esoterica. So, my disposition starts as favorable to great measurement.

Probably no other topic, however, invokes so much passion among teachers, students, and parents as grading, assessments, tests, and scoring. Diane Ravitch (2015) claims that "sometimes the most brilliant and intelligent minds do not shine in standardized tests because they do not have standardized minds," and Larry Strauss (2023) observed, "standardized testing has sucked the life out of learning. Stop focusing on test scores." On the other hand, Michelle Rhee (2011) stated, "Testing isn't about putting pressure on teachers or students. It's about ensuring that every child gets the same shot at learning and that teachers have clear metrics to help them improve their practice." And from Michael Barber (2017), "We use data to drive results, to identify what works and what doesn't. Tests can be an essential tool to make sure no child is left behind."

Along come Dave Nagel and Bruce Potter. Their major argument in this book is that when we use tests and grades in schools to improve learning by helping teachers and students see their impact on learning, we move toward nirvana: the impact of what we have taught (or learned) well or not, who we have taught (or have learned) well or not, and how much improvement there has been from our teaching (or learning). I see ten major messages in this book:

1. **Grades as Feedback, Not Final Judgments:** Grades should guide students in understanding their progress and identifying areas for improvement, supporting a learning journey rather than serving as definitive assessments.

2. **Clarity and Transparency:** Teachers and students benefit from clear learning goals, success criteria, and transparent grading practices, which foster a shared understanding of expectations and help students track their progress accurately.

3. **Emphasis on Learning Over Compliance:** Shifting away from a culture of compliance—where completing tasks is valued over actual learning—helps ensure that grades reflect real understanding and mastery rather than simple completion.

4. **Formative and Growth-Oriented Mindset:** Effective grading supports ongoing learning rather than marking an endpoint. This formative approach encourages students to see grades as feedback to guide the next steps.

5. **Constructive Feedback and Support:** Focusing on actionable feedback helps students address challenges, manage frustration, and view mistakes as learning opportunities, fostering resilience and self-regulation.

6. **Redefining Traditional Grading Practices:** Moving away from practices that can misrepresent learning, such as penalizing missed assignments harshly or averaging grades, helps ensure that grades more accurately reflect student progress and skill development.

7. **Collaborative Grading for Consistency:** Teacher collaboration in PLCs helps build consistency in grading, ensuring shared standards across classrooms and reducing variability in assessment practices.

8. **Flexible and Supportive Approaches:** Allowing multiple opportunities for students to succeed, using amnesty days, and offering targeted support (like MEAEC sessions) ensures that all students have a fair chance to meet learning goals, reinforcing a growth mindset.

9. **Personalized Success Criteria and Goal Setting:** Clear, mastery-oriented success criteria enable students to set realistic, challenging goals and strive for personal bests, which builds motivation and focuses them on learning.

10. **Teachers as Facilitators of Learning:** Teachers play a vital role in helping students evaluate and adjust their learning processes, creating a classroom culture that supports visible, assessment-capable learners.

And yes, I asked ChatGPT to help me with this top ten list. And there within lies the greatest change in my lifetime as a measurement academic. Within a few years, we will reflect on our overuse of multiple-choice questions and ask, "Why did we do this?" We will look back on the time we spent writing items and assessment questions and ask, "Why did we spend so much time doing this?" We will look back on scoring open-ended items, essays, and assignments and ask, "Why did we spent so much time doing this?" These advances (many are working hard on these issues right now) will *not* mean we are redundant. It will mean we can spend more time engaging in quality control and interpreting the results' meanings for our teaching and learning. Students will be able to integrate the best next steps to advance their learning. We will ask much more interesting items. We will create more aligned rubrics and scoring templates. We will spend less time creating and more time using and interpreting the scores from assessments. We will be able to use tests in the ways outlined throughout this book. Assessment will return to the service of improving learning, improving instruction, and improving where best to move next. Grades will be seen more as feedback to be heard, understood, and actioned, and there will be greater clarity and transparency.

As in the Visible Learning research, the major aim throughout the book is *how we think* as educators about assessment: It is less about what we do and more about how we think about what we do—and this also applies to assessment and grading. Gavin Brown (2004) has conducted a long and deep study of teachers' conceptions of assessment and noted four major themes: assessment as improvement (enhancing teaching and learning processes); assessment as student accountability (holding students responsible for their learning outcomes); assessment as school accountability (demonstrating the quality of schools and teachers; and assessment as irrelevant. It is the first core conception of assessment, and Witter (2024) has demonstrated that students give higher evaluations to teachers who use assessment for improvement.

A major contribution of this book is showing the tight nexus between assessment as improvement and the power of feedback. Grades are a form of feedback. But given the variability of feedback—one-third of feedback can be of no or negative influence (Kluger & deNisi, 1996)—the details outlined in this book help ensure that the feedback interpretations made by teachers or students is correct, understood, and actionable. After completing the grading and assessment, it is worth asking, "What did we learn about our impact so that we know best where to move next?" If we cannot answer this question, maybe the exercise was of limited to no use? We also need to ask, "Did we make accurate interpretations?" and if not, question the scoring quality, the alignment of the items to the curriculum concepts we wished to focus on, or whether the assessment rubric was good enough. We need to ask, "Are my students (and me) willing and keen to see errors, mistakes, and wrong answers as opportunities to learn or as embarrassments?" Following the book's theme, if there are no assessment consequences, we should take serious pause!

The messages about how we think about assessment and grading are powerful, and with the AI revolution that will reduce the workload of creating, scoring, and analyzing tests and measures, we can spend our professional skills on better aligning, interpreting, and learning from assessments—as teachers and as students. Visible learners will be the greatest beneficiaries of these ways of thinking about assessment.

References

Barber, M. (2017). How to deliver improved outcomes for school systems. *Qatar Organization*. wise-qatar.org

Brown, G. T. (2004). Teachers' conceptions of assessment: Implications for policy and professional development. *Assessment in Education: Principles, Policy & Practice, 11*(3), 301–318.

Kluger, A. N., & DeNisi, A. (1996). The effects of feedback interventions on performance: A historical review, a meta-analysis, and a preliminary feedback intervention theory. *Psychological Bulletin, 119*(2), 254.

Ravitch, D. (2015, February 19). Mercedes Schneider: The act bombshell blows up the myth of New Orleans "Reforms." [Web blog post]. http://dianeravitch.net/2015/02/19/mercedes-schneider-the-act-bombshell-blows-up-themyth-of-new-orleans-reforms/

Rhee, M. (2011). The evidence is clear: Test scores must accurately reflect students' learning. *Huff Post*. https://www.huffpost.com/entry/michelle-rhee-dc-schools_b_845286

Strauss, L. (2023). Standardized testing has sucked the life out of learning. Stop focusing on test scores. *USA Today*. https://eu.usatoday.com/story/opinion/voices/2023/09/21/test-scores-standardized-testing-bad-measure-education-learning/70856233007/

Witter, M., & Hattie, J. (2024). Can teacher quality be profiled? A cluster analysis of teachers' beliefs, practices and students' perceptions of effectiveness. *British Educational Research Journal, 50*(2), 653–675.

References

Bibliography:

Absolum, M. (2006). *Clarity in the classroom* (pp. 76–95). Hodder Education.

Ainsworth, L. (2011). *Rigorous curriculum design: How to create curricula units of study that aligns standards, instructions, and assessment.* Lead and Learn Press.

Allan, B. M., & Fryer, R. G. (2011). *The power and pitfalls of education incentives.* Hamilton Project.

Almarode, J., Fisher, D., & Frey, N. (2021). *How learning works. A playbook.* Corwin.

Almarode, J., Fisher, D., & Frey, N. (2022). *How feedback works. A playbook.* Corwin.

Ames, C. (1992). Achievement goals and the classroom motivational climate. In D. H. Schunk & J. L. Meece (Eds.), *Student perceptions in the classroom* (pp. 25–57). Lawrence Erlbaum.

Antonetti, J., & Stice, T. (2018). The work of school. In J. Antonetti & T. Stice (Eds.), *Powerful task design: Rigorous and engaging tasks to level up instruction* (pp. 7–26). Corwin. https://doi.org/10.4135/9781506399164

Bandura, A., & National Institute of Mental Health. (1986). *Social foundations of thought and action: A social cognitive theory.* Prentice-Hall.

Berry, A. (2022). *Reimagining student engagement: From disrupting to driving.* Corwin.

Biggs, J. B. (2014). Constructive alignment in university teaching. *HERDSA Review of Higher Education, 1,* 5–22.

Biggs, J. B., & Collis, K. F. (1982). *Evaluating the quality of learning: The SOLO taxonomy (structure of the observed learning outcome).* Educational psychology series.

Bloom, B. S. (1984). The 2 sigma problem: The search for methods of group instruction as effective as one-to-one tutoring. *Educational Researcher, 13,* 4–16. https://doi.org/10.3102/0013189X013006004

Bolam, R., McMahon, A., Stoll, L., Thomas, S., & Wallace, M. (2005). *Creating and sustaining professional learning communities.* Research Report Number 637. General Teaching Council for England, Department for Education and Skills.

Boonk, L., Gijselaers, H. J., Ritzen, H., & Brand-Gruwel, S. (2018). A review of the relationship between parental involvement indicators and academic achievement. *Educational Research Review, 24,* 10–30. https://doi.org/10.1016/j.edurev.2018.02.001

Brookhart, S. M. (1991). Grading practices and validity. *Educational Measurement: Issues and Practice, 10*(1), 35–36. https://doi.org/10.1111/j.1745-3992.1991.tb00182.x

Brookhart, S. M. (2008). *How to give effective feedback to your students.* ASCD.

Buell, J. (2004). *Closing the book on homework: Enhancing public education and freeing family time* (p. 176). Temple University Press.

Butler, D. L., & Winne, P. H. (1995). Feedback and self-regulated learning: A theoretical synthesis. *Review of Educational Research, 65*(3), 245–281. https://doi.org/10.2307/1170684

Butler, R. (1988). Enhancing and undermining intrinsic motivation: The effects of task-involving and ego-involving evaluation on interest and performance. *British Journal of Educational Psychology, 58,* 1–14.

Butler, R., & Nisan, M. (1986). Effects of no feedback, task-related comments, and grades on intrinsic motivation and performance. *Journal of Educational Psychology, 78,* 210–216.

Carless, D. (2006). Differing perceptions in the feedback process. *Studies in Higher Education, 31*(2), 219–233.

Castro, L. N. G., Hadjiosif, A. M., Hemphill, M. A., & Smith, M. A. (2014). Environmental consistency determines the rate of motor adaptation. *Current Biology, 24*(10), 1050–1061.

Cavanagh, S. (2003). Study: Teens' unfamiliarity with college demands is seed of failure. *Education Week Magazine.* https://www.edweek.org/teaching-learning/study-teens-unfamiliarity-with-college-demands-is-seed-of-failure/2003/03

Chesebro, J. L., & McCroskey, J. C. (1999). The relationship between students' reports of learning and their actual recall of lecture material: A validity test. *Communication Education, 49*, 297–301. https://doi.org/10.1080/03634520009379217

Chew, S. L., & Cerbin, W. J. (2020). The cognitive challenges of effective teaching. *The Journal of Economic Education, 52*(1), 17–40.

Clinton, J., & Hattie, J. (2013). New Zealand students' perceptions of parental involvement in learning and schooling. *Asia Pacific Journal of Education, 33*, 324–337. https://doi.org/10.1080/02188791.2013.786679

Cognard, A. M. (1996). *The case for weighting grades and waiving classes for gifted and talented high school students.* University of Connecticut, National Research Center on the Gifted and Talented.

Cooper, H. (2001). Homework for all--in moderation. *Educational Leadership, 58*(7), 34–38.

Crisp, G. T. (2007). Is it worth the effort? How feedback influences students' subsequent submission of assessable work. *Assessment and Evaluation in Higher Education, 32*, 571–581.

Danielson, C. (2007). *Enhancing professional practice: A framework for teaching* (2nd ed.). Association for Supervision and Curriculum Development (ASCD).

Dehaene, S. (2018). *How we learn: Why brains learn better than any machine . . . for now.* Viking Press.

Dollard, J., & Miller, N. E. (1950). *Personality and psychotherapy: An analysis in terms of learning, thinking, and culture.* McGraw-Hill.

Duckworth, A. (2016). *Grit: The power of passion and perseverance.* Scribner.

Dunlosky, J., Rawson, K. A., Marsh, E. J., Nathan, M. J., & Willingham, D. T. (2013). Improving students' learning with effective learning techniques: Promising directions from cognitive and educational psychology. *Psychological Science in the Public interest, 14*(1), 4–58. https://doi.org/10.1177/1529100612453266

Feldman, J. (2018). *Grading for equity: What it is, why it matters, and how it can transform schools and classrooms.* Corwin.

Feldman, J. (2020). Taking the stress out of grading. *ASCD.* https://ascd.org/el/articles/taking-the-stress-out-of-grading

Fendick, F. (1990). *The correlation between teacher clarity of communication and student achievement gain: A meta-analysis* [Unpublished doctoral dissertation]. University of Florida, Gainesville.

Fisher, D., Frey, N., Ortega, S., & Hattie, J. (2024). *Teaching students to drive their learning: A playbook on engagement and self-regulation, K-12.* Corwin.

Freeman, S., & Parks, J. W. (2010). How accurate is peer grading? *CBE—Life Sciences Education, 9*, 482–488. https://doi.org/10.1187/cbe.10-03-0017

Frey, N., Fisher, D., & Hattie, J. (2018). Developing "assessment capable" learners. *Educational Leadership, 75*, 46–51.

Friedman, S. J. (1998). Grading teachers' grading policies. *NASSP Bulletin, 82*(597), 77–83.

Goldberg, K. (2007, April). *The homework trap.* Paper presented at the Annual Meeting of the American Educational Research Association, Chicago.

Grant, D., & Green, W. B. (2013). Grades as incentives. *Empirical Economics, 44*(3), 1563–1592.

Green, T. F. (1971). *The activities of teaching.* McGraw-Hill.

Guskey, T. R. (2009). *Practical solutions for serious problems in standards-based grading.* Corwin.

Guskey, T. R. (2015a). *Grading and reporting student learning.* http://www.4aplus.com/wp-content/uploads/2015/02/41-Tom-Guskey-Handout.pdf

Guskey, T. R. (2015b). *On your mark: Challenging the conventions of grading and reporting.* Solution Tree.

Guskey, T. R. (2018). *Multiple grades: The first step to improving grading & reporting.* https://tguskey.com/multiple-grades-final-step-improving-grading-reporting/

Guskey, T. R. (2019, September). *Don't get rid of grades: Change their meaning & consequences.* https://tguskey.com/dont-get-rid-grades-change-meaning-consequences/

Guskey, T. R. (2020). *Breaking up the grade.* http://www.ascd.org/publications/educational-leadership/sept20/vol78/num01/Breaking-Up-the-Grade.aspx

Guskey, T. R. (2021). Learning from failures: Lessons from unsuccessful grading reform initiatives. *NASSP Bulletin, 105*(3), 192–199.

Guskey, T. R. (2022). Can grades be an effective form of feedback? *Kappan, 104*(3), 36–41. https://kappanonline.org/grades-feedback-guskey/

Guskey, T. R. (2023). *Implementing mastery learning* (3rd ed.). Corwin.

Guskey, T. R. (2024, April). Addressing inconsistencies in grading practices. *Kappan.*

Guskey, T. R., & Bailey, J. M. (2001). *Developing grading and reporting systems for student learning.* Corwin.

Guskey, T. R., & Bailey, J. M. (2009). *Developing standards-based report cards.* Corwin.

Guskey, T. R., & Brookhart, S. M. (Eds.). (2019). *What we know about grading: What works, what doesn't, and what's next?* Association for Supervision and Curriculum Development.

Guskey, T. R., Frey, N., & Fisher, D. (2024). *Grading with integrity.* Corwin.

Hanover Research. (2013). *Replacing "zero" grading at the secondary level.* http://dumais.us/newtown/blog/wp-content/uploads/2013/08/Hanover_ReplacingZeroGrading.pdf

Harackiewicz, J. M. (1979). The effects of reward contingency and performance feedback on intrinsic motivation. *Journal of Personality and Social Psychology, 37*(8), 1352–1363. https://doi.org/10.1037/0022-3514.37.8.1352

Harackiewicz, J. M., Manderlink, G., & Sansone, C. (1984). Rewarding pinball wizardry: Effects of evaluation and cue value on intrinsic interest. *Journal of Personality and Social Psychology, 47*(2), 287–300. https://doi.org/10.1037/0022-3514.47.2.287

Hattie, J. (2009). *Visible learning: A synthesis of over 800 meta-analyses relating to achievement.* Routledge.

Hattie, J. (2012). *Visible learning for teachers: Maximizing impact on learning.* Routledge.

Hattie, J. (2015). *What works best in education: The politics of collaborative expertise.* Pearson. https://www.pearson.com/content/dam/corporate/global/pearson-dot-com/files/hattie/150526_ExpertiseWEB_V1.pdf

Hattie, J. (2023). *Visible learning: The sequel: A synthesis of over 2,100 meta-analyses relating to achievement.* Routledge.

Hattie, J., & Donoghue, G. M. (2016). Learning strategies: A synthesis and conceptual model. *Npj Science of Learning, 1,* 16013. https://doi.org/10.1038/npjscilearn.2016.13

Hattie, J., & Timperley, H. (2007). The power of feedback. *Review of Educational Research, 77*(1), 81–112.

Hattie, J., & Zierer, K. (2017). *10 mindframes for visible learning: Teaching for success* (1st ed.). Routledge. https://doi.org/10.4324/9781003430124

Henderson, N. (2013). Havens of resilience. *Educational Leadership, 71*(1), 22–27.

Jenkins, L. (2021). Education's greatest challenge: Children start their education full of enthusiasm, but as they progress that enthusiasm fades badly. *Education Today.* https://www.educationtoday.com.au/news-detail/Education-5477

Jensen, E. (2000). Moving with the brain in mind. *Educational Leadership, 58,* 34–37.

Kiper, M. (2023). 2023 NFL draft grades for all 32 teams: Mel Kiper's steals, sleepers. *ESPN.* https://www.espn.com/nfl/insider/draft2023/insider/story/_/id/36187303/2023-nfl-draft-grades-all-32-teams-mel-kiper-steals-sleepers-favorite-picks-classes

Kirschenbaum, H., Simon, S. B., & Napier, R. (1971). *Wad-Ja-Get?: The grading game in American education.* Hart.

Kluger, A. N., & DeNisi, A. (1996). The effects of feed-back interventions on performance: A historical review, a meta-analysis, and a preliminary feedback intervention theory. *Psychological Bulletin, 119*(2), 254–284.

Lang, D. M. (2007). Class rank, GPA, and valedictorians: How high schools rank students. *American Secondary Education, 35*(2), 36–48.

MacDonald, R. (1991). Developmental students processing of teacher feedback in composition instruction. *Review of Research in Developmental Education, 8*, 1–4.

Marzano, R. (2006). *Classroom assessment and grading that work*. Association for Supervision and Curriculum Development.

McCall, R. B., Evahn, C., & Kratzer, L. (1992). *High school underachievers*. Sage.

McMillan, J. H. (2001). Secondary teachers' classroom assessment and grading practices. *Educational Measurement: Issues and Practice, 20*(1), 20–32. https://doi.org/10.1111/j.1745-3992.2001.tb00055.

McMillan, J. H., Myran, S., & Workman, D. (2002). Elementary teachers' classroom assessment and grading practices. *The Journal of Educational Research, 95*(4), 203–213.

Nagel, D. (2008). Giving high school students more time. *Principal Leadership, 8*(7), 29–31.

Nagel, D. (2015). Standards-based grading. In D. Nagel (Ed.), *Effective grading practices for secondary teachers* (pp. 167–204). Corwin. https://doi.org/10.4135/9781483386379

Najarro, I. (2024a). Grades and standardized test scores aren't matching up. Here's why. *Education Week*. https://www.edweek.org/teaching-learning/grades-and-standardized-test-scores-arent-matching-up-heres-why/2024/10

Najarro, I. (2024b). The new digital SAT: 4 important details educators need to know. *Education Week, 43*(18), 14. https://www.edweek.org/teaching-learning/the-new-digital-sat-4-important-details-educators-need-to-know/2024/01

Nicol, D. J., & Macfarlane-Dick, D. (2006). Formative assessment and self-regulated learning: A model and seven principles of good feedback practice. *Studies in Higher Education, 31*, 199–218. https://doi.org/10.1080/03075070600572090

Nuthall, G. A. (2007). *The hidden lives of learners*. New Zealand Council for Educational Research.

O'Connor, K. (2009). *How to grade for learning, K–12* (3rd ed.). Corwin.

O'Connor, K. (2010). *A repair kit for grading: Fifteen fixes for broken grades* (2nd ed.). Pearson Education.

O'Connor, K. (2017). *How to grade for learning: Linking grades to standards* (4th ed.). Corwin.

Oettinger, G. S. (2002). The effect of nonlinear incentives on performance: Evidence from "ECON 101". *The Review of Economics and Statistics, 84*(3), 509–517.

Page, E. B. (1958). Teacher comments and student performance: A seventy-four classroom experiment in school motivation. *Journal of Educational Psychology, 49*(4), 173–181.

Pauly, M. (2009). *One principal's self-study: Facilitating collaborative analysis of student work to inform teaching and learning* (UMI No. 3372099) [Doctoral dissertation, State University of New York at Buffalo]. ProQuest Dissertations and Theses database.

Perkins-Gough, D. (2013). The significance of grit: A conversation with Angela Lee Duckworth. *Educational Leadership, 71*(1), 14–20.

Popham, W. J. (2008). *Transformative assessment*. Association for Supervision and Curriculum Development.

Programme for International Student Assessment (PISA). (n.d.). *About PISA*. https://www.oecd.org/en/about/programmes/pisa.html

Prothero, A. (2023, February). What would motivate teens to work harder in school? The chance to redo assignments. *Education Week*. https://www.edweek.org/leadership/what-would-motivate-teens-to-work-harder-in-school-the-chance-to-redo-assignments/2023/02

Reeves, D. B. (2004). The case against the zero. *Phi Delta Kappan, 86*, 324–325. https://doi.org/10.1177/003172170408600418

Reeves, D. B. (2009). *Leading change in your school: How to conquer myths, build commitment, and get results*. ASCD.

Reeves, D. B. (2011). Data: Meaningful analysis can rescue schools from drowning in data. *Creative Leadership Solutions*. https://www.creativeleadership.net/resources-content/data-meaningful-analysis

Sadler, P. M., & Good, E. (2006). The impact of self- and peer-grading on student learning. *Educational Assessment, 11*(1), 1–31.

Schinske, J., & Tanner, K. (2017). Teaching more by grading less (or differently). *ASCB*. https://www.lifescied.org/doi/10.1187/cbe.cbe-14-03-0054

Scouller, K. (1998). The influence of assessment method on students, learning approaches: Multiple choice question examination versus assignment essay. *Higher Education, 35*, 435–472. https://doi.org/10.1023/A:1003196224280

Stanger-Hall, K. F. (2012). Multiple-choice exams: An obstacle for higher-level thinking in introductory science classes. *CBE Life Sciences Education, 11*, 294–306. https://doi.org/10.1187/cbe.11-11-0100

Starch, D., & Elliott, E. C. (1912). Reliability of the grading of high school work in English. *School Review, 20*, 442–457. https://doi.org/10.1086/435971

Sullivan, P., Knott, L., & Yang, Y. (2015). The relationships between task design, anticipated pedagogies, and student learning. In A. Watson & M. Ohtani (Eds.), *Task design in mathematics education* (pp. 6–8*)*. New ICMI Study Series. Springer.

Swanson, H. L. (1990). Influence of metacognitive knowledge and aptitude on problem solving. *Journal of Educational Psychology, 82*(2), 306–314. https://doi.org/10.1037/0022-0663.82.2.306

Swinton, O. H. (2010). The effect of effort grading on learning. *Economics of Education Review, 29*(6), 1176–1182.

Teach.com. (2017). *Homework around the world.* https://teach.com/resources/homework-around-the-world/

Titsworth, S., Mazer, J. P., Goodboy, A. K., Bolkan, S., & Myers, S. A. (2015). Two meta-analyses exploring the relationship between teacher clarity and student learning. *Communication Education, 64*(4), 385–418. http://search.proquest.com.er.lib.k-state.edu/docview/1773220800?accountid=11789

Topping, K. (2008). *Peer assisted learning: A practical guide for teachers.* Brookline Books.

Topping, K. (2020, August 27). *Peer tutoring and cooperative learning.* Oxford Research Encyclopedia of Education.

Towns, M. H., & Robinson, W. R. (1993). Student use of test-wiseness strategies in solving multiple-choice chemistry examinations. *Journal of Research in Science Teaching, 30*, 709–722.

Trautwein, U., Köller, O., Schmitz, B., & Baumert, J. (2002). Do homework assignments enhance achievement? A multilevel analysis in 7th-grade mathematics. *Contemporary Educational Psychology, 27*, 26–50. https://doi.org/10.1006/ceps.2001.1084

Vatterott, C. (2009). *Rethinking homework: Best practices that support diverse needs.* Association for Supervision and Curriculum Development.

Vatterott, C. (2014). Student-owned homework. *Educational Leadership, 71*(6), 39–42.

Welsh, M. E., & D'Agostino, J. (2009). Fostering consistency between standards-based grades and largescale assessment results. In T. R. Guskey (Ed.), *Practical solutions for serious problems in standards-based grading* (pp. 75–104). Corwin.

Wheeless, L. R. (1975). An investigation of receiver apprehension and social context dimensions of communication apprehension. *The Speech Teacher, 24*(3), 261–268. https://doi.org/10.1080/03634527509378169

Wiliam, D. (2016, April). *The secret of effective feedback.* https://www.ascd.org/el/articles/the-secret-of-effective-feedback

Winne, P. H., & Butler, D. L. (1994). Student cognition in learning from teaching. In T. Husen & T. Postlewaite (Eds.), *International encyclopedia of education* (2nd ed., pp. 5738–5745). Pergamon.

Wormeli, R. (2006). *Fair isn't always equal: Assessing & grading in the differentiated classroom.* Stenhouse; National Middle School Association.

Wright, J. (2006). Learning interventions for struggling students. *Education Digest, 71*(5), 35–39.

Yazzie-Mintz, E. (2010). *Charting the path from engagement to achievement: A report on the 2009 High School Survey of Student Engagement.* Indiana University, Center for Evaluation and Education Policy. https://www.scirp.org/reference/referencespapers?referenceid=2382321

Zoeckler, L. (2005). *Moral dimensions of grading in high school English* [Doctoral dissertation, Indiana University]. https://scholarworks.iu.edu/dspace/bitstream/handle/2022/7144/umi-indiana-1163.pdf?sequence=1

Index

Accuracy, 23, 43, 77, 89, 140–41, 189
Advanced Placement (AP), 63, 124
Agreement, 37, 140, 180, 182, 187
Amnesty days and periods, 128–29, 148, 150, 154, 160–62, 164–66
Arguments, 70, 79–81, 83, 102–3, 105, 111, 120–21, 144, 174
Assessments, 4, 10–11, 15–17, 27–28, 51–52, 55–57, 59, 63–64, 72–73, 80–81, 89–92, 132, 138, 172, 188–89
   capabilities, student, 11
   common, 35–36
   evidence, 47, 96, 102
   formative, 81, 158
   standardized, 63
   tools, 60–61
   and task grading matrix, 26, 29, 171
Assignments, 4–5, 7, 9, 22, 25–29, 37, 39, 65, 93–95, 129–30, 150–52, 154, 158, 162–65, 177–78, 186
   adjusted, 93
   busywork, 27
   challenging, 63, 164
   extra, 4–5
   missing, 160–61
   scoring to focus on progress, 110
Autonomy, 73, 157

Busywork, 158, 163, 165, 186

CGSG (Clarity of Grading Scoring Guide), 55–64, 77–78, 110–11, 140, 143, 174–75, 188
Change agents, 51–52, 56, 74, 78
Clarity
   teacher, 15, 18, 49, 55, 84, 188
   of grading scoring guide. *See* CGSG
Classwork, 26, 75–76, 130, 150, 154, 162, 171
Coasting, 26, 28–29, 94, 102

Collaboration, 7, 19, 22, 28–29, 36, 39, 164, 169–70, 178, 187, 189
   effective, 37, 179
   teacher, 29, 33–34, 38, 48, 52, 187
   collaborative learning, 77, 158, 169, 173
   collaborative scoring and collaborative feedback, 33, 188
   collaborative teams, 6, 14, 36, 114, 164, 188–89
   collaborative time, 41
Common Core, 179
Completion, 7, 18, 28, 63, 155, 158–59, 163–64, 170
   compliance, 6–7, 72, 155–56, 158, 163–64, 170
Complexity, 58, 60–61, 63, 162, 188
Confidence, 49, 52, 77, 87–88, 139, 188
   in students, 87
Continuous improvement, 28, 52, 74, 190
Core practices, 29, 34, 37–40, 42, 92, 99, 102, 133, 179
Counterpoints, 25–26, 72, 88, 112, 125–26, 131, 151, 168
Credit, 7, 95, 97–98, 110, 163

Davis High School, 161
Denominators, 31, 135–37, 139–40
Dialogue, 36, 51–52, 56, 109, 111, 114, 133, 150, 170, 175
Disabilities, 152, 176
Drafts, 66, 107, 109–10
Drivers, 6, 11, 30, 52, 86, 92, 106, 153, 173
   for mastery, 86–87

Engagement, 49, 177
English teachers, 65, 85
Environment, supportive, 52, 153, 165, 187. *See also* Supportive learning environment
Essays, 7, 69–70, 107, 109–11, 116, 120–21
   argumentative, 69, 81, 107, 110, 120–21
   final, 107, 110, 117

Evaluators, 50–52, 56, 74, 78, 187
Evidence, 6–8, 10–11, 34, 42, 45–47, 60–61, 63, 79–80, 90, 96–97, 101–3, 110–11, 114–17, 138, 164–65, 180–82, 186–87
   effective use of, 115, 117
   eliciting student learning, 18
   essential learning, 58
   generation, 60
   qualitative, 90
   student voice, 114
   and support, 108, 111

Failure
   fear of, 151, 153–54
   student, 46–48, 160
Fear, 31, 46
Formative mindset, 6, 8
Fractions, 31, 135–37, 139–40
Framework, 30, 34, 48, 55, 58, 62
Frustration, 69, 75, 86, 118, 150–53, 163
   student, 148, 151

Games, 6, 8–9, 29, 138
Generative learning experiences, 56–57, 60–62, 78, 111, 143, 175
GPA (grade point average), 24, 148
Graphic organizers, 28, 69–70, 82, 107–11
Growth
   personal, 49, 149, 186
   student, 39, 64

High school, 24, 45, 75, 85, 95, 124, 148, 166. *See also* Wonder
   coursework, 63
   students, 95, 118, 148, 156
Homework, 7, 26–27, 47, 75–76, 81, 102, 150, 154–60
   assignments, 24, 60
   deliberate practice element of, 24
   effectiveness of, 156, 160
   focus of, 155
   grading, 155
   impact of, 150, 154
   legitimate purpose for, 160
   parent surveillance of, 157
   practice tasks, 155
   support for short frequent, 156
   using, 148

Independent learning skills, 159
IP (in progress), 97–98, 100–101, 119–21

Language, 85, 116, 160
   of learning, 51–52, 56, 150, 170, 175
Laws, 23, 142–43
   common and positive, 143–44

Math teachers, 65, 85, 105
MEAECs (Missing Essential Assignments Extended Chance), 28, 47, 148, 154, 162, 164–66
Meetings, 35–36, 65, 85–86, 135, 137, 139, 142
Meta-analyses, 13–14, 50, 132
Middle school, 45, 69, 92, 123, 152, 163, 171, 178. *See also* Wonder
   students, 78, 104, 179
Mindsets, 6–8, 10, 31, 46, 52, 124, 126, 128, 131
   grading, 126, 131
Misconceptions, 31, 83
Monitoring, 34, 37, 74, 150, 154–55, 158–59
Motivation, 15–16, 46–47, 151–53, 168, 174
   student, 42, 189

NME (no mastery evidence), 120–21

Objectives, 8, 11, 52, 78, 143, 175
Outcomes, 38, 49, 59, 76
Outlines, 82, 111, 115–17, 142

Parents, 3, 5, 7, 10, 21, 23, 38, 40, 64–65, 75–76, 97–98, 123–24, 147, 155–56, 158–59
   and students, 38, 64–65, 97–98, 101, 119
   support for autonomous student behavior, 157
   surveillance, 157
PBL (Project-Based Learning), 57
Peer
   feedback, 19, 174, 176–77
   grading tasks, 28
   self-assessment, 177
   tutoring, 169, 173, 177
Penalties, 19, 43, 47, 128, 160–62, 165
Perfectionism, 150–51, 153–54
PISA (Programme for International Student Assessment), 45
Planning, 59, 70, 105, 151, 188
PLCs (professional learning community), 14, 22, 34, 36, 38–39, 61–62, 65–67, 83, 85, 130, 155–56, 158, 164, 186, 189
   on grading and feedback, 164
   leads, 65–66
Precipice of Cognitive Challenge, 63, 78, 111, 143–44, 175
Presentations, 23–24, 28, 44, 60, 69–70, 83, 144, 180–81

Problems, 16, 47, 57, 63, 85, 105, 158
    solving tasks, 125, 138
Professional learning community. *See* PLCs
Proficiency, 23, 37, 42–43, 46, 97–98, 100, 118–19, 134–36, 141
Programme for International Student Assessment (PISA), 45
Project-Based Learning (PBL), 57
Punishment, 151

QR Codes, 39, 160

RA (receiver apprehension), 153
Reflection journals, 159, 174
Reflective practices, 113, 159
Relationships, 51–52, 56–57, 78, 87–88, 128, 143
Reliability, 40, 61, 63, 93
Resilience, 47, 80
Responsibilities, 43, 129, 151, 164
Reteaching, 37, 161, 171–72
Rewards, 138
Rigor, 7, 48, 58, 61–63, 76–77, 162, 187–88
Rubrics, 91, 115–16, 128, 134, 138, 168, 174, 176–77, 183
    single point rubrics (SPRs), 128, 134, 137–39

Safety, 45
Schoolwork, 118, 123
Science, 75–77, 79–81, 105, 124, 152, 175
    teachers, 65, 76, 85, 165
Second chances, stipulated, 33–34, 37, 42–44, 48, 130–31, 188

Self-grading, 177–79
Single point rubrics (SPRs), 128, 134, 137–39
Social studies, 65–66, 75–76, 120, 178
    teachers, 65–66, 69, 171
SPRs. *See* single point rubrics
Standards, 37, 40, 62, 76, 81, 99, 105, 115
Struggling students, supporting, 164
Success criteria, 19, 21, 34–35, 37, 72–73, 91–95, 97–99, 102–4, 106, 109–10, 125, 133–36, 168, 176–77, 186–87
    using, 36, 86–87, 106, 121
Supportive learning environment, 10, 64, 88, 95. *See also* Environment, supportive

Teamwork, 28, 168
Thesis statements, 108, 111
Topic sentences, 108, 111
Training tasks, 28, 109, 113, 118, 120–21
    initial, 120
    ungraded, 119
    use of, 113, 121
Traits
    of students, 11, 18, 21, 51, 73, 150
    of visible learners, 14, 44, 48, 51, 164, 187
Trust, 34, 51–52, 56, 64, 87–88, 128, 143

Visiblelearningmetax.com, 115, 132

Wonder
    High School, 76, 95, 102, 107, 119, 142, 179
    Middle School, 40, 65, 82, 99, 115, 120–21, 165, 173
Worksheets, 28, 82

Build your Visible Learning® library!

TEACHER CLARITY

GREAT LEARNERS BY DESIGN

GREAT TEACHING BY DESIGN

LEARNING TO LISTEN AND LISTENING TO LEARN

THE ILLUSTRATED GUIDE TO VISIBLE LEARNING

VISIBLE LEARNING: THE SEQUEL

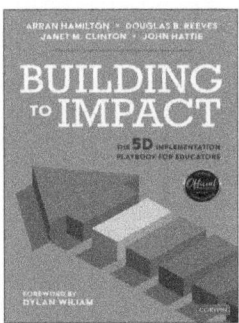
BUILDING TO IMPACT

MAKING ROOM FOR IMPACT

COLLECTIVE STUDENT EFFICACY

Order your copy at corwin.com

CORWIN

Helping educators make the greatest impact

CORWIN HAS ONE MISSION: to enhance education through intentional professional learning.

We build long-term relationships with our authors, educators, clients, and associations who partner with us to develop and continuously improve the best evidence-based practices that establish and support lifelong learning.